DAUGHTERS OF DIGNITY

DAUGHTERS OF DIGNITY

AFRICAN WOMEN IN THE BIBLE AND THE VIRTUES OF BLACK WOMANHOOD

LaVerne McCain Gill

The Pilgrim Press

Cleveland, Ohio

The Pilgrim Press, Cleveland, Ohio 44115
© 2000 by LaVerne McCain Gill

Printed in the United States of America on acid-free paper

05   04   03   02   01   00   5   4   3   2   1

Library of Congress Cataloging-in-Publication Data

Gill, LaVerne McCain, 1947–
    Daughters of dignity : African women in the Bible and the virtues of black
womanhood / LaVerne McCain Gill.
        p. cm.
    Includes bibliographical references and index.
    ISBN 0-8298-1373-X (paper : alk. paper)
    1. Virtues—Biblical teaching.   2. Blacks in the Bible.   3. Women in the Bible.
4. Afro-American women—Conduct of life.   5. Afro-American women—
Religious life.   I. Title.

BS680. V56 G55   2000
277.3'0082—dc21

                                                                            99-057376

to

Mary McCain Williams, my mother

Clement R. Williams, my stepfather

Dr. Tepper L. Gill, my husband

Paul McCain and John McCain, my brothers

Dylan McCain McDuffie and Tepper McCain Gill, my sons

Dorian McDuffie and Jennette Hardy, my stepdaughters

in memory of

Frederick Sterling McCain, my brother

Lilly Thornton, my grandmother

Paul McCain, my father

Contents

Acknowledgments

On November 20–21, 1997, the first class of the course "African American Women in the Ministry: The Church's Role in Reclaiming the Virtues of Womanhood" was held at Princeton Theological Seminary's Center of Continuing Education. The participants in that program included lay leaders, founders of churches, ministers, Christian educators, chaplains, and seminarians. It was the first time that many of the participants had attended a course of this nature. The two-day continuing education program not only provided the participants with tools to create new ministries for their churches, but it also offered an opportunity to explore the biblical, theological, and historical context within which African American women created an ethic of womanhood. The course book that I wrote for the seminar formed the basis for this book.

Any number of people deserve thanks for making it possible to turn that course book into this book. I will attempt to name a few of the people; any name left out is a matter of a lack of memory on my part, but not a lack of support and input on the parts of those involved.

First, I want to thank God for giving me the gift of writing and the ability to put into words what I have felt in my heart. Without divine help, I am truly helpless. Next, I want to thank my immediate family. My mother, Mary Williams, deserves a bouquet of flowers and a tearful thanks for always being there to wish me well and support me. I stand on a foundation made up of her ethics and faithful witness. I only hope that I have been able to be an exemplar of what she tried to teach me about being a child of God and an African American woman of faith. I am grateful for my stepfather, Clement Williams, who has been more than a father to me and has never stopped encouraging me to shoot for and reach the goal.

One person who deserves a prominent place and a debt of gratitude in all of this is my husband, Dr. Tepper L. Gill, whose brilliant mathematical mind has never gotten in the way of his ardent and passionate faith and belief in God. His steady faith and love undergird me at my weakest moments. My sons, Tepper and Dylan, continue to be beacons that make the future look and feel possible and brighter, just because they were born and exist. My two stepdaughters, Dorian McDuffie and Jennette Hardy, deserve recognition for carrying on the tradition of African American womanhood in their chosen professions and in their personal lives. I include with them my nieces, Marlene McCain and Kyana McCain, both of whom hold the promise and key to the future of black womanhood. A special note of thanks goes to my brothers, Paul and John McCain, who are vigilant and purposeful fathers and role models for their sons, Mark and Rashun McCain.

The initial course and the subsequent book would not have been possible were it not for some very key people. First of all, let me thank Dr. Joyce C. Tucker, dean of continuing education at Princeton Theological Seminary, for allowing this course to be taught at the center. Second, in the Princeton Theological Seminary community, I would also like to give a great deal of thanks to Dr. Peter J. Paris, Elmer G. Homrighausen Professor of Christian Social Ethics, and liaison with the Princeton University Afro-American Studies Program. Dr. Paris served as my thesis advisor and is a person to whom I owe a great deal of gratitude for his scholarly insight and his continued support. Dr. Katherine Doob Sakenfeld, W. A. Eisenberger Professor of Old Testament Literature and

Exegesis, and director of Ph.D. studies, invited me to lecture her class on the Queen of Sheba during the formative stages of this book, and I am appreciative of that experience for the insight it afforded.

It is certainly important to thank the women who participated in the first course and who provided their own experiences as a way of validating some of the suppositions about the ethics of black womanhood. They are Carmen Aiken, Aundreia Alexander, Rev. Sheila Bradshaw, Barbara Edmonds, Joanne Perez, Thelma Calbert, Barbara Flythe, Tawainna Houston, Estelle Johnson, L. Adelle Jones, Regina Langley, Diane Rouse, Conchita Showell, Rev. Hazel Staats-Westover, Florence Tate, Thomasina Washington, Mary Williams, Elizabeth deCastro, Blanche LaVere, Rev. Barbara Mungin, and Urla Eversley.

Additional thanks are extended to the distinguished Ghanaian theologian and professor Mercy Oduyoye, director of the Institute of African Women in Religion and Culture at Trinity Theological College, Accra, Ghana, for facilitating the session titled "African/African-American Women in Dialogue." Rev. Dr. Melinda Contreras-Byrd, a psychologist and A.M.E. elder, is due a thank-you for her session "Healing the Wounded Healers." A note of thanks is also extended to the participants in the worship service titled "Three African Women in the Bible: Their Virtues and Their Role in God's Salvific Plan," during which time I delivered sermons based on material in this book. The worship service participants were Jane Ferguson, Greg Jones, Cornel Edmonds, Luke Powery, Angela Lewis, Darnell Allen, Regina Langley, and Carmen Aiken.

Professionally, I want to thank my literary agent, Natasha Kern, of Natasha Kern Agency, for making it possible for me to write without worry or stress. To Kim Sadler, my acquisitions editor at United Church Press, I owe a great deal of gratitude for being patient and understanding throughout this publication process.

Many other names ought to be in these acknowledgments but do not appear, so to all those who have been left out, I thank you from the bottom of my heart. It is my hope that the finished product will be worthy of the support that was given to make the work on this book possible.

Introduction

SEVENTEENTH CENTURY: ON THE WAY FROM AFRICA:

It was his general practice on the receipt of a woman slave—especially a young one—to send for her to come to his cabin so that he might lie with her. Sometimes they would refuse to comply with his desires and would be severely beaten by him and sent below. . . . Female slaves had a fair idea of their fate and spent miserable hours in anticipation of it. The surgeon of the Ruby recalled hearing them sing sad songs about their former lives and lost countries.[1]

EIGHTEENTH CENTURY: ONCE IN AMERICA:

Perhaps most disturbing of all was the fact that many slave women felt they had no choice but to submit to a master's sexual demands. They were keenly aware that their families could be sold away from them at a moment's notice and that the punishment for resistance to a planter's advances was rape, flogging or even death. . . . Some of these women eventually took their own lives when their imaginations failed to provide them with any other means of escape from the lasting nightmare of rape.[2]

NINETEENTH CENTURY: AFTER SLAVERY:

Whereas the subscribers, women of color of the Commonwealth of Massachusetts, actuated by a natural feeling for the welfare of knowledge, the suppression of vice and immorality, and for cherishing such virtues as will render us happy and useful to society, sensible of the gross ignorance under which we have too long labored, but trusting, by the blessing of God, we shall be able to accomplish the object of our union—we have therefore associated ourselves under the name of the Africa-American Female Intelligence Society.[3]

TWENTIETH CENTURY: AFTER THE CIVIL RIGHTS MOVEMENT:

But I think first of what is in this that's going to push black America. We need that push. We needed it since we came over here packed like spoons in the slave ship. And here we are now sitting in the halls of Congress. What has God wrought? What has he wrought? What has he wrought?—Congresswoman Carrie Meek (D-Fla.)[4]

How did African women transform themselves into today's African American women? What was the process that they used to reenvision their lives as women of God and not slaves of men? How did they move from the mantle of oppression to the altar of praise; from the bottom of the slave ship to the halls of Congress? What is their link to the stories of African women in the Bible? What can oppressed women around the world learn from the faith journeys of African American women?

Daughters of Dignity: African Women in the Bible and the Virtues of Black Womanhood does not attempt to answer all these questions, but it does look at one way in which African American women reinvented, redefined, and reclaimed their womanhood in the aftermath of slavery. By seizing upon Christian virtues as the basis for the formation of character, African American women forged an ethic of black womanhood that defined the manner in which they would survive in an alien and strange land—America.

A historic snapshot of nearly four centuries of black women reveals that they were able to forge dignity out of degradation and hope out of despair, not only for themselves, but also for their families and their race. By uplifting Christian virtues and clinging to a boundless faith, they measured their value and worth in God's human family.

Daughters of Dignity, an outgrowth of a seminar held at Princeton Theological Seminary's Center of Continuing Education, examines five Christian virtues in light of two groups of women—African women in the Bible and African American women. It emphasizes African American women's reliance on the virtues of justice, love, faith, wisdom, and perseverance that are evident in the stories of Hagar, Zipporah, Rahab, the Queen of Sheba, and the Canaanite woman. By employing these five virtues, African biblical women shared in the unfolding of God's plan for redemption and salvation. Whether they gained knowledge through the biblical stories or in the course of crafting a life out of the depravity of slavery, African American women also employed these virtues and others. These virtues formed the basis of a womanhood ethic that has served generations of black women.

Just as Rahab, the prostitute, used faith and courage to re-create and redefine herself as a new woman in the promised land of Canaan, so, too, have many African American women transformed themselves into new women in America. In many instances, black women had to restructure the biblical stories taught by white preachers and slave owners in order to carve out a message that reaffirmed their humanity and protected the essence of who they were as women of God. In so doing, they have had to devise distinctive reading strategies for their study of the Bible.[5]

Reading the Bible Using a Justice Reading Strategy

Daughters of Dignity adds to these reading strategies by introducing a new one—*a justice reading strategy.* This strategy grows out of the literary tradition. More specifically, it comes from looking at the impact of African biblical women and their role in God's unfolding salvation story as it is reflected in the Bible and the extrabiblical historic and sacred literature of the surrounding cultures of Egypt, Mesopotamia, Canaan, and Ethiopia. Since the Hebrew text has as its focal point the story of the Israelite cultures, those people surrounding them are sometimes viewed as having no place in God's plan for salvation. Understanding how the role of non-Israelites is interpreted by their own traditions and how they impact and produce new insights into the Hebrew Scriptures is the aim of this more holistic approach to biblical studies. Called a justice reading strategy because of God's option for the oppressed and the disinherited, this approach seeks to point to the work of God in the world to all of humanity—male and female, Hebrew and non-Hebrew. Thus, it assumes that God is a God of all people. It assumes that the chosen Hebrew people were able to draw from the surrounding cultures because those cultures had also formulated praise and thanksgiving to the God who had performed miracles in their lives. Consequently, while the Hebrew story is the foundation for the Judeo-Christian faith, it does not preclude the presence of God in the lives of others and God's intentional movement in the world to bring about a salvation for the whole world. When we employ this strategy, African biblical women are lifted out of the footnotes of biblical history and placed in the salvation story.

An example of the way in which I have employed this justice reading strategy can be found in the story of the Queen of Sheba. In this book, I look at the story of the Queen of Sheba as she appears in the Hebrew narrative, and I also attempt to look at the *Kebra Nagast* and what the Ethiopian tradition celebrates about the Queen of Sheba (Queen Makeda) and how this story transformed the religious, political, and social culture of Ethiopia up until the twentieth century.

By employing a justice reading strategy, we may discern the salvific role of these African women who surrounded and intermarried with the Hebrew people. This justice reading strategy unmasks women whose very purpose is integrated into the historical faith narrative of the ancient world. They are not merely footnotes in salvation history as feared by Dr. Renita Weems when she wrote: "Dutifully, we sat through sermons, lectures, and Bible study lessons, nodding when appropriate, copiously taking notes when expected and, when called upon, obediently recapitulating what we have been told. All the while our souls have remained starved for a new revelation on the role of women in salvation history. Surely, God did not mean for us to be a footnote to redemption."[6] The justice reading strategy ensures that such a fate does not befall African biblical women.

Objectives of the *Daughters of Dignity*

Like the seminar upon which it is based, *Daughters of Dignity* has four objectives: (1) to provide new insights into Christian virtues as reflected in the stories of African women in the Bible; (2) to place this new information in the context of the history of African American women and their intentional attempts at creating an ethic of black womanhood; (3) to encourage the exploration of personal faith journeys; and (4) to create new reading strategies for the Bible. It is anticipated that with the accomplishment of these objectives women will be encouraged to create and design new and more radical women's discipleship ministries as well as deepen their own spiritual understanding.

Why Write a Book about the Virtues of African Biblical Women and African American Women?

In May 1955, weeks before her death, educator and activist Mary McLeod Bethune wrote what she called her legacy to the next generation. In it she said, in part: "I leave you love. . . . I leave you hope. . . . I leave you the challenge of developing confidence in one another. . . . I leave you a thirst for education. . . . I leave you respect for the use of power. . . . I leave you faith. . . . I leave you racial dignity. . . . I leave you a desire to live harmoniously with your fellow man. . . . I leave you finally, a responsibility to our young people."[7]

The words of Mary McLeod Bethune and the many other women who had guarded the image of black women and girls were reminders of the responsibility of each generation to its youth. The poignancy of Bethune's words were brought into full focus when an article appeared several years ago in the *Washington Post* about welfare reform.

On the front page of the Sunday, October 19, 1997, issue of the *Washington Post* there appeared a young African American woman, age fifteen, sitting on a sofa with her thumb in her mouth, her hair un-combed, wearing a T-shirt, a nine-month-old baby hanging between her legs. The caption read: "Generations of Pain: Denise Jordan Is Off Welfare and Loves Her Job. But What About Her Daughter?"

Such a picture provoked African American women to protest, as never before, the *Post*'s use of such imagery. It painted a picture of black women as poor, on welfare, hopeless, hapless, and lazy. Having spent seven months tracing this mother and daughter for the story, the pho-tographer used this front-page photograph after culling through numer-ous shots. By its own admission in a later op-ed ombudsman's column, the *Post* received unprecedented responses from black women who flooded its editors with letters, complaints, and phone calls. One woman who attended the Princeton seminar said she called the editor, the re-porter, the photographer, and the ombudsman before the paper re-sponded. Why were these African American women angry?

First of all, they knew the statistics. The U.S. Census Bureau in 1994 counted 25.4 million poor whites and 10 million poor blacks. There are more white women than black women on welfare, and nearly twice as many white as black children are growing up in poverty. Rather than view the issue of poverty as one of social justice that requires work on the parts of the society and the church, it appeared to some of these women that the newspaper chose to contribute to racial stereotyping by choosing these particular photographs.

Second, they knew that black women had been used by the media as the face of welfare, the cause for reform, and the symbol of all that was wrong with poverty in the United States. These women were tired of being bombarded with media images of black women as prostitutes, crack addicts, unfit mothers, and pariahs of the system. While severe so-cial problems existed among all poor people, black as well as white, Latino, and American Indian, the stereotypes presented by the press were almost always black women. The women who protested were re-viving the battles that had been fought by Bethune and others who pushed to gain respect for the image of womanhood that had been so elusive. It was in many ways a wake-up call for African American women that the struggle continued.

Before and during Dr. Bethune's generation, black women were on the front lines promoting race pride and attempting to uphold the virtues of womanhood. However, those women no longer existed as beacons of womanhood for young women. Perhaps that is why the article brought back for many African American women the recognition that something needed to be done to combat negative images and stories. They seem to have remembered the Bethune legacy.

During this same period, there was another woman who had not forgotten the Bethune legacy—Dr. C. Delores Tucker, president of the National Congress of Black Political Women. Tucker openly and aggressively attacked black rap music and the industry moguls for the misogynist language, the depiction of black women in sexually explicit clothing, the suggestive dancing on videos, and the references made to black women by the use of profanity. Tucker was the first to openly proclaim that there was, indeed, an ethic of black womanhood and that efforts to denigrate black women were contrary to the rich history of so many African American women's groups, organizations, and associations.

But for many, her words fell on unhearing ears because the link between the generations that promoted the virtues of perseverance, love, faith, wisdom, and justice had been broken. More than three decades of integration made black women less intentional about establishing an ethic for younger women. Moreover, the vehicles that once existed were no longer available or accessible to most young women. For example, sororities were in touch, for the most part, only with college-educated women; the National Council of Negro Women did not, as a rule, reach inner-city girls; and the YWCA systems were replaced by fewer social programs and more recreational facilities. Churches remained the mainstay for inner-city young women, but the connections between church life and social life were few.

Where would young black women regain the connection with their ethical roots? How would they hear the stories of strength, courage, and faith that propelled generations of black women into productive careers and strong families? *Daughters of Dignity* is an attempt to trace the biblical history and the theological history of these efforts in the hope that contemporary black women will find in this book a useful resource as they face the myriad of religious, social, and cultural problems in their faith journeys. It is also hoped that this book will capture the imagination of women who need to know and those who are seeking to find out how the church can reclaim these virtues and pass them on to the next generation.

Background: The Unique Faith Journey of African American Women

The enslaved African woman's transition into the twenty-first-century African American woman began in 1619 when seventeen African men and three African women were forcibly brought to Jamestown, Virginia. In 1624, a black male child named William was born to a woman known only as Isabella, becoming what would be the first legal slave born in America. Thirty-eight years later, Virginia law established that children born within the colony "would be held bond or free according to the status of the mother."[8]

This very ruling added to the complex existence of black women, complicating their lives as women, mothers, wives, and slaves. Black women faced a harsh reality—one that constituted a life lived out in contradictions. The most poignant was the practice of the Christian faith by white men and women.

For example, while Christianity was emerging as the religious tradition in America, black women had to reach into the depths of their own faith to endure the consequences of the daily contradictions of practicing Christians. They experienced the contradictions as they were raped by Christian plantation owners. They experienced the contradictions as they were ferried to America on slave ships with the name Jesus painted on the sides. They experienced the contradictions as Christian captains allowed men and women to lay in excrement and stench throughout the Atlantic voyage, while still others suffered abuse on the upper deck. They experienced the contradictions as they bore children whose

Christian fathers treated them as property and a source of investment and capital. They experienced the contradictions as black fathers were chained, sold, whipped, mutilated, or lynched by Christians. And they experienced the contradictions as they were required to nurse and love children of any and every color, including white Christian women's babies, as their own went hungry.

Black women lived with these contradictions, and yet they were the producers of generations that would make cotton king and America strong and prosperous. They were the breeders of laborers for the land, the workers, and the possessors of wombs whose economic value was amortized over a lifetime. In the midst of this, African American women had to eventually respond to a fundamental question of survival: "How is it possible for human beings to endure the terrible pressures of the dominating world without losing their humanity, without forfeiting their souls?"[9] The noted theologian Howard Thurman phrases the question in this way: "There is one overarching problem that the socially and politically disinherited always face: Under what terms is survival possible?"[10]

As with most human beings, black men and women had to respond to this question as soon as they were forcibly taken away from their homes and culture in Africa. For most, the response came in the manner in which they survived over the torturous years of slavery, the brutalization during the period following the Civil War, the destructive years preceding the civil rights victories, and the continued struggles in a post–civil rights era. Of particular note is the way that African American women answered the question. For them, the question of the quality and terms of survival also meant defining their womanhood.

While white women were being urged to be the symbol of chaste Victorian virtue, black women were being sexually abused and used to supply a labor force for the United States. Black women had been defined in the marketplace as commodities, not human beings. As a consequence, part of their survival meant that they were forced to develop their own internal worth and value. In order to do that, they had to ask themselves, What did it mean to be human? What did it mean to be a woman? What did it mean to be a black woman?

Nobel laureate Toni Morrison's award-winning novel *Beloved* explores some of these questions about the quality of survival.[11] The novel's tragedy begins with the brutalization and rape of a slave woman, Sethe. Pregnant and defenseless, she is unable to fight off the young white rapists who drain her humanity from her as they drink her breast milk. It is the ultimate attempt to deprive her of any dignity with an act so brutal, so haunting, that Sethe later kills her baby daughter, Beloved, when there is a threat of reenslavement.

It could be said that *Beloved* is a story about the tragic toll that slavery exacted on African American women. Yet the story proves to have intermittent triumphs as it depicts a slice of life of three generations of black women—Sethe, her mother-in-law, Sug, and her daughter, Denver—who traverse the American landscape trying to make sense out of their slave-era experience. While Sethe succumbs to her demons and ghosts, Sug becomes the spiritual healer of a generation of people, and Denver triumphs to go on into the world as a self-assured, wise, and courageous young woman. That a new generation might emerge and take hold of their own dignity and destiny is a subplot of *Beloved*, but it is the main story of African American women. For black women—a cult of women who shared the same plight in America—the question of survival was foremost, and the quality of that survival had to be intentionally structured and not left to chance. Questions had to be answered.

While Morrison answers some of these unasked questions, others remain. What type of black woman would emerge from the North American slave trade? How would she be able to survive the assault on her soul and her womanhood? What would she need to survive, intact and whole? How would she define her humanity, given the history of systemic inhumane treatment? What would she tell her daughters? And how would she embrace her religion? The way in which these questions were answered would determine the meaning of black womanhood and would form the foundation for an ethic of black womanhood. The proponents of the ethic of black womanhood also sought ways to transmit these virtues and values from one generation to another. Morally wounded from slavery, African American women leaders recognized that the formation of character would entail turning the vices of slavery on their heads and clinging to religious virtues. Every known civilization from the beginning of recorded time has developed guidelines for how members in the society should function with each other. African American women and men were no different. The boundaries they used were Christian beliefs, and their ethics were Christian ethics. The life of Jesus as well as the work of Jesus formed the basis for their paradigm.

What Are Christian Virtues?

Then someone came to him and said, "Teacher, what good deed must I do to have eternal life?" And he said to him, "Why do you ask me about what is good? There is only one who is good. If you wish to enter into life, keep the commandments." He said to him, "Which ones?" And Jesus said, "You shall not murder; You shall not commit adultery; You shall not steal; You shall not bear false witness; Honor your father and mother; also, You shall love your neighbor as yourself." (Matt. 19:16–19)

The young man was asking Jesus, What does it take to live a moral life? What are the virtues, the traits, that will make him eligible to become a citizen in the realm of God? According to some Christian teaching, virtue is a habit or a disposition of right conduct. Virtues may be acquired by education and repetition, or they may be infused. The virtues aimed at the perfection of human nature without respect to its supernatural end are called natural virtues. The virtues that have to do with a supernatural destiny are called supernatural or, in the Judeo-Christian tradition, theological virtues. Some virtues are thought to be acquired, and others are thought to be infused in the heart and soul by means of grace.[12]

Scripture identifies many virtues; chief among them are justice, faith, hope, charity (love), perseverance, wisdom, and courage. Most Christian writers identify three theological virtues—faith, hope, and charity (love)—but the others are mentioned throughout the Gospels, the Hebrew text, and the Epistles. "The theological virtues grow with grace and when they find expression in good works, merit further increase in grace."[13]

Black women organized around many of these Christian virtues and addressed moral conduct that would assure them of a place in God's created reality. They sought survival strategies that were necessary for the uplift of other women and men, and they sought justice. This is evident in the establishment of societies such as the Africa-American Female Intelligence Society of Boston (mentioned in the opening examples). Their preoccupation with morality and forging moral uplift came out of the need to overcompensate for the slavery experience. With African American women serving as the spoils of a conquered people, the need to intentionally move to a fuller understanding of self as a part of the created world of God was necessary for physical as well as spiritual survival.

They became a part of a long line of societies and peoples who sought to develop guidelines for moral conduct and faithful witness. For example, the sages of the Near Eastern civilizations had their moral codes, Mesopotamia had Hammurabi's code, while the Egyptians had their Book of the Dead. Judaism has the Torah with the Ten Commandments, Muslims have the Qur'an with the teachings of Muhammad, Buddhism has the teachings of Buddha, and Christianity has the life and proclamations of Jesus Christ.

While most of the major world religions view their virtues within a spiritual context, philosophers, on the other hand, have tried to define virtue outside the context of religion. Both philosophy and religion, however, tend to ask the question: What kind of person should a believer or adherent be? This question is important not just for the individual, but for the community as well. Christians found the answer in the life of Jesus and the witness of God's work in the world and history as evidenced in the Bible. African American women found their virtues in this biblical source as well.

Since virtues could be acquired by education and repetition or infused, African American women began educating each other about what it meant to be courageous, wise, faithful, loving, just, persevering, and hopeful. These Christian virtues and others became their mantra for the uplift of a race. These same virtues were also evident in the characteristics of African biblical women as their role in God's salvific plan unfolded in the stories of the Bible.

Connecting African American Women with African Biblical Women

Years ago, Dr. Cain Hope Felder wrote about the story of black women's survival. In the early 1980s Felder, the editor of the *Original African Heritage Study Bible* and a New Testament language and literature scholar and professor, authored an article entitled "The Bible, Black Women and Ministry." In that article, Dr. Felder challenged African American women scholars and writers to document the life of American black women, Third World women, and other women of color and to write about their life experiences and faith journeys by connecting with the stories of African biblical women. Felder also spoke of including in these stories "the themes of uplift and liberation and divinely-inspired leadership . . . and the identification and reclamation of African women in the Bible who are preeminently identified as progenitors of the black woman of today in terms of her low estate circumstance, enormous faith, and responses to opportunities to exercise ministerial leadership."[14]

He cautioned, however, that while telling the stories of African American women and their faith journeys might not be difficult, identifying and using the stories of African biblical women might prove to be more of a challenge because the images in the Bible were still assumed to be European. This, despite the fact that the historical evidence did not support the claim.

For example, the activity in the Hebrew Scriptures (Old Testament) clearly takes place in what we now call Africa, while the Gospels and the life of Jesus unfold in what we now call the Middle East, but what is actually northern Africa. Unraveling the history and the geography is a part of the challenge that Felder makes to women writers. Of course, much of his research in later years would prove to be the foundation upon which any such writings would depend. Nevertheless, he states that the task is especially difficult because of the changing concepts of race:

Our task would be extraordinarily difficult, if not hopeless, if we restricted our purview to those few women in the Bible who, by modern standards of racial typology, might be considered black, for example, the Cushite (Nubian) wife of Moses (Num. 12); the Queen of Sheba (1 Kings 10; 2 Chronicles 9) to whom New Testament writers later refer as "the Queen of the South" (Matthew 12:42; Luke 11:31) or the Kandanke Queen of the Nubians of Mero (Acts 8:27). . . . The bible does not provide us with concepts of race that are commensurate with modern standards for so-called racial types.[15]

Felder does conclude, however, that because there is a link between women of color and the presence of African bloodlines, it is possible to use these clearly identified women in addition to others to develop a scriptural basis for connecting African American women to these biblical stories. Felder was not the first to call for this type of writing. What is important about his articulation of the issue is the fact that he was and remains a major force within academia, whose focus has been on establishing a foundation for identifying the African presence in the Bible. He has authored and/or edited such groundbreaking works as *Troubling Biblical Waters*[16] and *Stony the Road We Trod*[17] as well as written numerous scholarly articles pioneering, openly postulating, and affirming the African Asiatic roots of the Hebrew Scriptures and the Christian Scriptures. *Daughters of Dignity* is one attempt to respond to Felder's challenge.

Organization of the Book

Following this introduction, the book is organized into five parts and a conclusion. Each part deals with one of the five virtues—justice, love, faith, wisdom, and perseverance. Within each part are three chapters. The first chapter gives a brief definition of the virtue, pointing to its biblical context. Within the chapter is a discussion of one African American woman whose life, work, or writings exemplify that virtue.

The chapter that follows the first provides a detailed look at the story of an African biblical woman's role in God's unfolding salvation plan.

The woman's reliance on the virtue identified is an integral part of this analysis. This chapter includes scriptural references, retells the Bible story, and offers an overview of the traditional interpretations of the narrative. What is new is the introduction in this chapter of a justice reading strategy that highlights the African biblical woman's role in God's salvation story for humanity.

Reflection questions make up the final chapter in each part. These questions include biblical references to the virtue presented, as well as questions that probe deeper into the points raised in the chapter.

The conclusion presents ways in which the book might be used in mentoring programs, in retreats, and in creating new women's ministries. It calls upon the reader to employ personal insight in assessing the contemporary issues that impact black women and consider ways in which to establish new strategies for using the church to reclaim these virtues for the furtherance of an ethic of black womanhood. This renewed emphasis on the intentional creation of an ethic of black womanhood has the potential of producing creative ministries, outreach efforts, and strategies for a new generation of women. It also has the potential for revitalizing efforts designed to address some of the social problems facing African Americans that may lead to the strengthening of families and communities.

Daughters of Dignity offers an opportunity to gain new insight into the stories of African biblical women and to develop a linkage between their stories and the spiritual history of African American women. Yet while African American women have a unique experience, their plight is shared by many women today. The spiritual paths of women who have been victims of slavery or war carry some of the same scars—children born out of rape who in many instances share two cultures or two races, strained relationships between the sexes, a loss of self-worth and self-definition, and a search for ways to redefine womanhood that take into account the injustices suffered. Whether it is the story of African American women and their faith journey through American slavery, segregation, and civil rights or Bosnian, Albanian, Tutsi, or Korean women, the plight of women who are considered the spoils of war remains the same. They are left to make sense out of who they are after the devastation and dehumanization. They are left to answer the question raised by Howard Thurman: "Under what terms is survival possible?" Many black women answered that question by seeking solace in the biblical stories that affirmed their humanity and by looking at the intrinsic virtues of womanhood and not arbitrary societal definitions. Historically, the latter denied them a place in the world of women; the former strengthened them in their resolve to create an ethic of womanhood that acknowledged their struggles and their value as women of God. It is hoped that this book will affirm for black women their rich ethical legacy and provide guidance for other women who suffer, even today, from the same tragedy of oppression, abuse, and dehumanization by Christians and non-Christians alike who continue to engage in domination and war.

part one

JUSTICE

God has taken God's place in the divine council;
  in the midst of the gods God holds judgment:
"How long will you judge unjustly
  and show partiality to the wicked?
Give justice to the weak and the orphan;
  maintain the right of the lowly and the destitute.
Rescue the weak and the needy;
  deliver them from the hand of the wicked."
They have neither knowledge nor understanding,
  they walk around in darkness;
  all the foundations of the earth are shaken.
I say, "You are gods,
  children of the Most High, all of you;
nevertheless, you shall die like mortals,
  and fall like any prince."
Rise up, O God, judge the earth;
  for all the nations belong to you! (Ps. 82:1–8)

Justice as a Virtue and Rosa Parks

The scene in Psalm 82 symbolizes a turning point in the cosmic debate between the gods of the Near Eastern cultures and the one God of Israel. It is a pivotal point in the divine council because it separates the God of the Israelites (capital "G") from the other gods (small "g") by the nature of their relationship with the poor, the orphan, the widowed, and the oppressed. The one God, Elohim, is distinguished by a concern for the weak and the needy. The psalmist makes it clear that giving justice to the outcast, oppressed, and poor is a prerequisite for maintaining divine standing in the council. By the end of Psalm 82, only one God emerges, immortal and divine, while the others are condemned to "die like mortals, and fall like any prince" (v. 7).

From this and other passages in the Bible, the biblical meaning of justice emerges. Justice—maintaining the right relationship to the lowly and the destitute, rescuing the weak and the needy, and delivering them from the hand of the wicked—was and remains one of the most significant attributes of God (vv. 3–4). It naturally follows that made in the image of God, human beings are called to seek justice as a desirable virtue. Consequently, the Hebrew word *mishpat* (justice) is not only an attribute of God, but also a virtue for men and women to cultivate as they respond to the call of God. It is a call that beckons them to include in the human circle those who have been left out and locked out.

From the Bible, three meanings of justice can be discerned: justice as an attribute of God; justice as a characteristic to be sought after by men and women; and justice as the quality of the relationship that should exist among human beings living in community.[1] Whether it is the Golden Rule, the Ten Commandments, the Beatitudes, the Prophets, or the words of Jesus, the message of justice resonates throughout the Scriptures as God's requirement for human beings and God's rationale for intervening in the world on their behalf.

Justice formulates the foundation for the statement that "God has an option or preference for the poor and oppressed." The theological foundations for both the Hebrew Scriptures and the Gospels are God's option for the poor and disinherited, along with love and righteousness. It is God's mandate for humanity to establish right relationships with the oppressed in society. The Exodus story about the deliverance of the Israelites from bondage and the Gospel message flowing from the life of Jesus affirm God's message "to let the oppressed go free" (Luke 4:18).

"Remember that I brought you out of the land of Egypt with an outstretched hand" is God's constant refrain to the Israelites. Providing the poor and oppressed with assurance of deliverance was an ethical mandate of the cultures surrounding the Hebrews as well. For example, predating the Hebrews is the ancient Egyptian expectation of justice—*Ma'at*.

> At the heart of the Egyptian ethic was *Ma'at*, a word that signified justice, balance, the norm, order, truth, what is correct and right action, all of which were established in the beginning by the gods and were presently guaranteed by the pharaoh. . . . No law codes defining Ma'at have been recovered and the concept appears to have functioned as a basic value providing the foundation for moral behavior and judgment. . . . Justice and truth were not

vague concepts, they were to be spoken and lived. . . . Individual Egyptians were expected to operate in harmony with Ma'at, not in terms of prescribed legal precepts, but rather broadly and freely, although in later times the tendency was to form rules.[2]

From the pre-Hebrew cultures of the Egyptians and Mesopotamians up to the life of Christ as portrayed in the Gospels, justice as a virtue was an enduring theme. In the Gospels, this virtue is the foundation of the Christian mandate in Matthew 25:35–40: "'For I was hungry and you gave me food, I was thirsty and you gave me something to drink.' . . . 'And when was it that we saw you a stranger and welcomed you, or naked and gave you clothing? And when was it that we saw you sick or in prison and visited you?' And the king will answer them, 'Truly I tell you, just as you did it to one of the least of these who are members of my family, you did it to me.'"

This sense of justice causes God to intervene in human history, demonstrating through the Israelites how it is to be meted out in the world. Justice is the lesson taught by the life of Jesus as he includes in his ministry the outcasts and the left out. Justice is an attribute of God and an aspiration of the followers of God. God exacts justice when the Hebrews are delivered from the land of Egypt, and God exacts justice when Jesus is born, crucified, and resurrected for the sins of the world.

Justice, then, is both a mandate from God for humanity and a characteristic of God in relationship with humanity.

From the Latin *jus* (right or law), the word "justice" has not only a biblical definition, but also a philosophical and secular definition. Where Plato defined it as the supreme virtue of the state, Aristotle separated the definition into two parts, distributive and retributive justice. Distributive justice was "one's just share of the resources of the state; and retributive justice, [meant getting] redress of injury."[3]

What is lacking in the philosophical meaning, however, is the significance of love to the dispensing of justice. The acclaimed African theologian Saint Augustine (354–430 C.E.) defines justice as "love serving only the loved object, and therefore ruling rightly."[4]

For Augustine, all of the Christian virtues begin with the love of God. Throughout the Bible, the call of God to humanity is not only to love God, but to do justice—judge rightly other human beings and worship God in earnest. Most theologians agree with Augustine that the foundation of justice is love, unselfish agape love. The prophet Micah considered justice to be a mandate of God. He wrote,

> *He has told you, O mortal, what is good;*
> *and what does God require of you*
> *but to do justice, and to love kindness,*
> *and to walk humbly with your God? (Mic. 6:8)*

In the American experience, Martin Luther King Jr. preached justice and love, turning a country and a world around and changing hearts and minds, freeing the oppressed. Whether African Americans in the United States or former East Germans in Europe, King's clarion call for a more inclusive and just society made an impact on the world. It was justice that Martin Luther King Jr. demanded during the civil rights movement when he defended his nonviolent strategy for achieving freedom from segregation and discrimination. The self-described drum major for justice called the United States to its highest moral self when he petitioned the world to take note of the injustices of segregation and discrimination:

> Finally, the method of nonviolence is based on the conviction that the universe is on the side of justice. It is this deep faith in the future that causes the nonviolent resister to accept suffering without retaliation. He knows that in his struggle for justice he has cosmic companionship. This belief that God is on the side of truth and justice comes down to us from the long tradition of our Christian faith. There is something at the very center of our faith which reminds us that Good Friday may reign for a day, but ultimately it must give way to the triumphant beat of the Easter drums. . . . So in Montgomery we can walk and never get weary, because we know that there will be a great camp meeting in the promised land of freedom and justice.[5]

In looking at African American women's response to injustice, we must remember that had not Rosa Parks sat down on the bus, Martin Luther King Jr. may never have stood up for justice. King's fight for justice began with the refusal of a black woman to give up her seat to a white man on a Montgomery, Alabama, bus. Rosa Parks's insistence upon justice and respect sparked a movement to end oppression and to bring equity, parity, and justice to African Americans. Rosa Parks (1913–   ), a hardworking seamstress and respectable citizen, could no longer endure the injustice of segregated public transportation, and on that day in December 1955 she became the woman who would later be referred to as the mother of the civil rights movement.

Following her lead and act of courage, a young preacher and reluctant prophet took up the cause for justice in Montgomery, along with other local clergy and ordinary black citizens. A year later, after a bus boycott and national protests that led to the U.S. Supreme Court's ruling declaring segregation in public accommodations unconstitutional, the framework for the civil rights movement of the 1960s was established. King, who was catapulted into the national headlines, would later say that had it not been for Rosa Parks, the civil rights movement might not have gotten started in quite that way. Parks was special in more ways than one. An established community leader, she was a woman respected for her demeanor and character who had integrity that could not be questioned when whites began to criticize the protests.

Rosa Parks was actually the third black woman in Alabama to refuse to give up her seat on the bus to a white person. In her book of poetry entitled *On the Bus with Rosa Parks,* the former American poet laureate Rita Dove pays tribute to the two other women who preceded Parks. The two women, Claudette Colvin and Mary Smith (now Ware), were memorialized in Dove's poems "The Enactment" and "Claudette Colvin Goes to Work." In "The Enactment," Dove reinforces the point that Mrs. Parks was an ideal person to ignite a protest because of her character. She was a married woman, respected in the community. Such a volatile situation would not have been well served, according to Dove, by a teenager such as Mary Smith. Dove paints a picture of Mary Smith as a poor teenager whose standing in the community would be subject to question and ridicule.[6]

Although Dove's poetry may be an overstatement of the issues confronting those ready to take on the system, Parks nevertheless was a distinctly well-suited candidate for the test—so well suited that her act of civil disobedience as a protest against an unjust law led to one of the most successful and morally grounded social justice movements of the twentieth century. It was a movement for justice that was achieved through nonviolent means and a theology that embodied agape love. This blueprint for justice would be used in the succeeding decades—a time when the conscience of the United States and the world would be challenged and the hearts of a nation circumcised.

Rosa Parks's impatience with injustice had been brewing for years. On several occasions she had complained to her employers about the segregation in Montgomery, prompting them to support her when she was invited to be a part of a training class at the controversial Highlander Folk School in Tennessee. The school, when Parks attended it in 1955, was a training ground for labor organizers and activists and itself a victim of harassment by the federal government.

Labeled by the FBI as a training ground for socialists and radicals, Highlander represented something quite different for the adult Rosa Parks. More than being affected by the school's program, she was affected by the atmosphere of racial integration that had been Highlander's hallmark since 1944 when it began integrating its student body. Of the school's multiracial staff and participants, Parks remarked, "That was the first time I had lived in an atmosphere of complete equality with the members of the other race."[7]

Rosa Parks's activism predated her time at Highlander, however. A member of the National Association for the Advancement of Colored People (NAACP), Parks came from a socially active and conscious family. Fighting for justice was a part of the legacy that she inherited from her mother, who fought for equal pay for black teachers in Alabama.[8]

Perhaps the example of her mother's activism set the stage for Parks's courageous catalytic action. Her nonviolent protest launched a movement that set the tone for an era of nonviolent resistance against injustices. From the South to the North—civil rights, antiwar, feminist protests—nonviolent demonstrators created history in the most militarily powerful country in the world. The movement had a worldwide stage, and others followed in the path. Whether it was the peace movement in the United States or the Berlin Wall in Germany, a force for justice had been unleashed that changed the second half of the twentieth century. It was a century in which the name Rosa Parks would become a historic symbol in the fight for justice and social transformation through an active principle of love.

Her life threatened, her job security diminished, Rosa Parks was not deterred. She would live to see the fruits of her courageous act in legally desegregated public facilities, high schools, colleges, and workplaces. She would also live to see the assassination in 1968 of Martin Luther King Jr., the drum major for justice. It was the end of an era that began with a woman deciding to take control of her destiny and moving a country closer to justice for African Americans. It was a blueprint for justice.

In the following story of Hagar, a biblical blueprint is available, one in which God intervenes in history to exact justice. This Egyptian slave, who encountered God in the wilderness and received a promise that her oppression would end and her son would be the father of nations, is an exemplar of God's divine intervention on behalf of the oppressed. Both Hagar and Rosa Parks represent women of color integrally involved in liberating acts of courage—acts designed to fight injustice.

The Story of Hagar: God's Blueprint for Justice

Scripture Readings

The following are biblical references to Hagar. Read them before beginning this chapter.

- The first story of Hagar: pregnant with Abraham's child, Hagar flees to the wilderness and meets God there (Gen. 16:1–16).

- The second story of Hagar: cast out by Abraham and Sarah, Hagar, destitute, thirsty, and hungry, encounters God again in the wilderness (Gen. 21:8–21).

- God promises Abraham that Ishmael will inherit a people, but not those chosen by God for deliverance (Gen. 17:17–21).

- Both Abraham and Ishmael are circumcised (Gen. 17:23–27).

- Ishmael and Isaac are reunited at the death bed of Abraham (Gen. 25:7–11).

- The descendants of Ishmael are listed (Gen. 25:12–18; 1 Chron. 1:28–31).
- Paul uses the Hagar/Sarah story as an allegory to distinguish between being born of the spirit and being born of the flesh (Gal. 4:21–31).
- The writer complains that Hagar's children, the Ishmaelites, did not know the way of wisdom (Bar. 3:23).

Introduction

This sketch is written for the good of those that have written and prayed that the slaves might be a freed people and have schools and books and learn to read and write for themselves and the Lord, in his love for us and to us as a race, has ever found favor in His sight, for when we were in the land of bondage, he hears the prayers of the faithful ones and came to deliver them out of the land of Egypt. For God loves those that are oppressed and will save them when they cry unto Him, and when they put their trust in Him.[1]

These words come from a slave narrative about the belief in a God of freedom.

Given the history of American enslavement of Africans, it is easy to see how African American women can identify with Hagar—probably more than any other African biblical woman. Her story, in large measure, parallels their historical narrative—sexual abuse as a vulnerable African slave, mistreatment at the hands of slaveholding wives, resentment by the slave's mistress because of children born of her husband, and fear of inheritance of whatever kind.

These points are made clearly and forcefully in Delores Williams's book *Sisters in the Wilderness.* Williams, a womanist theologian, makes it known to a broad spectrum of readers that "Hagar's story offers a route to the issues affecting Black women," issues that grow out of their unique American experiences as women caught up in the brutality of slavery and the subsequent attempts at their dehumanization.[2]

Up until Williams's exhaustive study, however, Hagar's story was generally overshadowed by the saga of Abraham and Sarah, the slaveholders rather than the slave woman. The plight of Hagar was seen a lot more readily by African American women, who historically sought refuge in the wilderness of everyday life in America in order to wait and hear the voice of God.

Hagar's story resembles that of black women in many ways. It is a story of a woman, like their ancestors, who is a servant in a household that deprives her of control of both her body and her life. It is a story where one woman's convenience becomes another woman's burden. It is a story where race and gender play roles in the oppression of one person over another. It is a story of a single mother who prays for the life of her son and receives God's promise of a better day. It is a story of a slave, pregnant with the master's child, who encounters God. But it is also a story of God's promise of two nations, to two brothers, one for the son of a slave woman and another, the son of a slaveholder. It is the story of a woman in the wilderness seeking justice and finding a God—El-roi— who sees her oppression and hears her cries for help and answers. In short, it is a story of God's justice.

New insights into Hagar's story continue to unfold, not only in the works of Williams, but also in the works of Old Testament scholars such as Dr. Renita J. Weems (author of *Just a Sister Away: A Womanist Vision of Women's Relationships in the Bible*)[3] and others who have breathed new life into the old story by providing fresh perspectives and new reading strategies coming out of the lived tradition of black women.

Coming from the African American womanist tradition, these women have created a new prism through which to view Hagar's experience with God. Williams in particular has provided what amounts to the most comprehensive commentary on Hagar, breaking new ground for interpretation and giving a popular audience a book that directly links this biblical passage to the historic and contemporary lives of African American women.

The remainder of this chapter will retell the story of Hagar, review her role in God's unraveling plan for salvation, present an overview of traditional commentaries, and using a justice reading strategy, look at the story as a part of a broader worldview as written about in the history of the Islamic and Arab community of believers.

The Story

In his old age, Abraham is promised by God that he will sire a son, who will be the father of a nation of people, blessed and chosen by God. Because of his age, Abraham laughs at the possibility that such a promise might come true. This promise to Abraham, despite the barrenness of his wife, Sarah, is an integral part of his covenant with God.

In the meantime, Sarah, impatient about God's promise, gives Abraham her slave girl, Hagar, to use as the mother of the promised child. Without any say in the matter, Hagar becomes the concubine of Abraham and conceives a child. Hagar is said to have become contemptuous of Sarah once she is pregnant, and for her apparent arrogance, Sarah mistreats her, forcing her to run away into the wilderness.

Historical notes reflect that Hagar's attitude may have been fostered by an understanding of the code of Hammurabi,[4] in which a pregnant maidservant's status is changed in the household once she conceives a child by the master of the household. In that code labeled Section 146, it states: "If a man takes a priestess, and she gives to her husband a maidservant, and she bears children and afterward that maid-servant would take rank with her mistress; because she has borne children her mistress may not sell her for money, but she may reduce her to bondage and count her among the female slaves."

Knowledge of this code may also contribute to Sarah's treatment of Hagar and Abraham's remark to Sarah that "your slave-girl is in your power; do to her as you please" (Gen. 16:6). When she hears this statement, the scripture records that Sarah treats Hagar harshly, causing her to run into the wilderness.

While in the wilderness, Hagar is discovered by an all-seeing God that she names El-roi. This name comes from the Canaanite tradition of placing a prefix "El" in front of a word to determine an attribute of God. Thus, Hagar calls God El-roi, "God sees." The Canaanite language, of which Hebrew is a dialect, uses the "El" prefix in a variety of names referring to God. For example, in Genesis 35:7, there is El-Bethel (God of Bethel); and in Genesis 14:18–20 we find El Elyon (God Most High).

It is the first time that God is given a name in the Bible, and it is the first time in the Hebrew Scriptures that a woman has such a theophany. Fearful of God, Hagar finds it hard to believe that she has seen God, face-to-face, and lived. But she not only sees God; she receives a blessing from this God she names El-roi. By way of instructions, she is told to return to Sarah and to deliver her child and name him Ishmael (God hears). This part of the narrative ends with the understanding that an all-seeing and all-hearing God will be with Hagar as she returns to an oppressive situation.

Ishmael is taken in by Abraham and accorded all the rights of a first-born, being circumcised along with his father at the behest of God and presumably being trained by Abraham to succeed him. Abraham petitions God to make Ishmael a part of the covenant, but God refuses. God remains true to God's original covenantal promise: the son of Sarah will become the leader of the nation of God's chosen people.

When Sarah eventually conceives as God had promised, she heightens her efforts to get rid of Hagar and Ishmael. The opportune time comes at the weaning ceremony for Isaac, Sarah's son. Sarah accuses Ishmael of mocking Isaac, although the translations differ on whether the two are playing harmlessly or whether Sarah's perceptions actually bear any relationship to the truth. Convinced that Ishmael and Hagar can damage her security and the inheritance of her son, Sarah orders Abraham to "cast out this slave woman with her son; for the son of this slave woman shall not inherit along with my son Isaac" (Gen. 21:10).

Thus, this time Hagar does not run away into the wilderness, but is sent there by Abraham at the behest of Sarah. Before obeying Sarah, Abraham first secures a promise from God that God will take care of Ishmael. He then sends Hagar and Ishmael away—seemingly with God's blessings—with a morsel of bread and not enough water. Destitute in the wilderness with her son and fearful that he will die, Hagar prays to God, and God hears the sobbing of Ishmael and comes to Hagar's aid with a well of water. Hagar is said to have lived in the wilderness of Paran with Ishmael until he was old enough to marry, at which time she sought a wife for him in Egypt (Gen. 21:21).

Ishmael is mentioned again when he and Isaac bury their father, Abraham (Gen. 25:9). The last mention of Ishmael is made of his offspring at his death, when the scripture lists his offspring (Gen. 25:12–18). Hagar is mentioned in allegorical form by Paul as he talks about the children of the one free in God and the children of the one enslaved by the flesh. "The children of the spirit" and "the children of the flesh" are the terms used to draw an analogy between those born in Christ (the spirit) and those born only in the flesh (Gal. 4:21–5:2). The only other reference to Hagar can be found in the apocryphal writings of Baruch, where wisdom is referred to as "Hagar's child." This oblique reference speaks more about the Ishmaelites than about the matriarch, Hagar.

Hagar's Role in Salvation History

The Hebrew people, similar to the communities that surrounded them— the Mesopotamians, the Egyptians, the Canaanites—saw justice (the caring for the oppressed, the orphan, and the widow) as a major attribute of their God, Yahweh. This story of Hagar's encounter with God in the wilderness is the quintessential story of such preunderstandings. Moreover, Hagar stands in the middle of all three traditions. An Egyptian by birth, she is brought to Canaan by Abraham and Sarah. In her union with Abraham she bears a child whose heritage is part Egyptian, part Mesopotamian. In her encounter with God she uses the Canaanite prefix "El" to name the God that she meets in the wilderness—El-roi (the God who sees). Transcending the Hebrew Scriptures, Hagar's story becomes the basis for a new culture, a new people, and a new religion. The Arab people celebrate their heritage as descendants from Ishmael, the son of Abraham and Hagar. They consider them the patriarch and matriarch of their people and the Islamic tradition and faith.

A new perspective on Hagar's story emerges by looking at God's plan for salvation for all people. Although she undergoes slavery and oppression, she is treated in the Bible as few women and men are treated. She is accorded the status and experience with God that only the patriarchs receive. Like Abraham, she is given a promise of a child who will father a nation. Like Moses, she sees God and names God. Like the Hebrew people, she is met in the wilderness by God and given sustenance and delivered from starvation. Like the Hebrew people during their oppression, she utters a cry heard by God, who knows of her affliction.

Hagar's story gives meaning to God's plan for deliverance of all people, not just the Israelites. This is borne out by the uniqueness of her story and the introduction of other cultural practices that come out of her encounters with God. They include the naming of God, the matriarchal implications in the scripture, and the unique role that she plays as a woman who receives God's attention and benefits from God's justice.

Hagar's first encounter is highlighted by the fact that she sees God and lives. Equally important is that, once seeing God, she names God El-roi. Nowhere else does this name appear in the Hebrew Scriptures, although this naming convention appears. The practice of using the prefix or suffix "El" accompanied by an attribute of God can be found in the references in the early books of the Bible reflecting a Canaanite naming custom. For example, El-Shaddai means God Almighty (Gen. 28:3; 35:11; 43:14; 48:3; Exod. 6:3; Ezek. 10:5), and El Elyon, God Most High (Gen. 14:18, 19, 20, 22); and of course, we find Immanuel, meaning "God is with us," in Isaiah 8:8.

Hagar is the only woman given the chance to name God. This may speak to the fact that the Hebrew culture was highly patriarchal, while the surrounding cultures, such as Egypt, though not perfect were more matriarchal and may have been more egalitarian. For example, it is said that Hagar selected a wife for Ishmael, but the custom of wife selection is generally a father's role in a patriarchal society. Both acts—the naming and the wife selection—imply that the story of Hagar and Ishmael may have its origin in another culture.

Hagar's story is set apart from other Hebrew Scriptures in other ways. One is the presence of a non-Hebrew nonmale receiving a blessing and a visit from God. Another is that God's compassion and God's promises extend beyond the Hebrews and that God's justice includes equality for women. In other words, a caring God exhibits compassion, promise, and presence in the world outside the chosen Israelites and particularly outside their patriarchal system. Not only is Hagar the only woman in the Hebrew Scriptures to receive such a theophany, but she also, like the patriarchs, is given a blessing and a promise of descendants and a nation from God. "Thus, Hagar is portrayed as the first genuine matriarch of the Old Testament. This North African woman, an Egyptian by birth, demonstrates that the divine promise could be given to a non-Israelite and a woman."[5]

Even if Hagar's role in God's plan for salvation ended with her place as the matriarch of a nation of people, it would be sufficient. Her story, however, serves other purposes. The narrative has symbolic meaning. Hagar is placed in the Genesis narrative to give validation to God's faithfulness to the covenant established with Abraham and to provide a blueprint for the way God works in the world to dispense justice.

The following interpretations of the scripture look at some of the structural and theological commentaries on the narrative.

1. The Two-Story Thesis

Commentators have speculated that the Hagar story is really two stories—one story in Genesis 16 and another story in Genesis 21. They point to the different personal characteristics of Hagar in the wilderness as evidence of two distinct stories.

For example, her first trip to the wilderness comes out of her refusal to stay and be mistreated by Sarah. Even Sarah's comments about her contemptuous attitude make her appear to be a spirited and defiant woman. By casting herself into the uncertain wilderness to keep from being abused, Hagar shows herself to be a woman with spunk and determination. "She is a bold, proud, resolute Egyptian woman who will not allow herself to be treated 'harshly' by her mistress. Here, upon becoming pregnant, Hagar assumes an air of equality with her mistress (v. 4)."[6]

Such spirited behavior is contrasted with her behavior in chapter 21, where Hagar is resigned to her plight in the wilderness and succumbs to the inevitability of death. This picture of an African woman giving up on her life and her son was deemed highly unlikely by the Ghanaian theologian Mercy Oduyoye. Oduyoye remarked that the image of an

African woman sitting under a tree, while her son is at a distance dying of thirst, defies the historical ethos of African mothers. Certainly, any image of starving African mothers and babies bears witness to this observation. Even when the milk is dry in the breast, the African mother can be seen holding the child and clinging to every last bit of life left. This perception is supported, in part, by the Arab historical narrative on Hagar. Indeed, as the story unfolds in the Arab tradition, Hagar climbs a mountain looking for water for her thirsty son.

With respect to the two-story thesis, Hebrew scholars believe that the second version (Gen. 21) may very well have been edited to reflect a more servile Hagar. In the second story, Hagar cries out to God, but God responds to Ishmael's cry and answers. Some feel that the hand of a more patriarchal redactor might have been at work in this part of the story, denying the possibility that God would speak directly to a woman or hear her cries. This two-story theory, however, is not held by all commentators. One feminist theologian sees the second story as a continuation of the first.

2. Hagar and the African American Woman's Issues

Commentary from womanist scholars, such as Delores Williams in *Sisters in the Wilderness,* focuses more on the person of Hagar and the "social, cultural realities relevant to the Biblical account." She does this to point to the meaning of the narrative from the "position of the slave woman, Hagar, rather than from the perspective of slave owners (Abraham and Sarah) and their culture."[7]

By recasting the story of Hagar in the context of the African American woman's historical encounters with slavery, Williams is able to frame African American women's issues in light of the plight of the Egyptian maidservant. Reading from the position of the oppressed allows her to look at the issue of justice from the recipients' end. In this respect, Williams explores four aspects of the Hagar story that relate to the black woman's experience: "the predicament of motherhood; the character of surrogacy; the problem of ethnicity; and the meaning and significance of wilderness experience for women and for the community."[8]

It is in these areas that Williams introduces a new interpretation of the scripture and provides valuable insight into the religious and quality-of-life survival ethos of African American women. She elaborates on what she has coined the "survival/quality-of-life tradition of African-American Biblical appropriation." This tradition, she says, is one that is "consistent with the Black American community's way of appropriating the Bible so that emphasis is put upon God's response to Black people's situation rather than upon what would appear to be hopeless aspects of African American people's existence in North America."[9]

The Hagar narrative, then, provides for this kind of interpretation as Hagar meets hopelessness with hope and promise when God is revealed to her in her time of need and destitution. Black women can relate to Hagar's single-mother's prayer for sustenance in the wilderness because they have borne witness to God's fulfilled promises for sons who may be "wild asses" of men, and they have faith journeys that reflect God's presence during their time of trial. An "all-hearing, all-seeing" God has been there for them and is the foundation, in most cases, for their faithfulness. They can find solace in the experiences of Hagar when she is pregnant in the wilderness and God promises a son, a future, and a relationship with God that is enduring.

"Name your son Ishmael," the all-seeing God tells Hagar, "God hears." This naming implies that God will be near and available. Black women also identify with Hagar's second encounter, when God performs a miracle, is true to the promise of hearing Hagar's and Ishmael's cries, provides water, and promises a nation to a slave woman and her son. These themes resonate with African American women who have been in the wilderness crying out at times when it was thought that "even hope was dead."[10] Although they did not receive the promise of a nation, they have borne children with aspirations and dreams of nation building.

3. Hagar's Story as a Blueprint for Justice

Commentators have pointed out that Hagar's story can be considered a blueprint for what is to come in the Hebrew Scriptures. It is the precursor to the Exodus story. This blueprint for justice is comprised of God's response to oppression at a point when God sees, hears, and acts with a blessing and a promise; but the promise of God comes with a recognition that life and the enduring struggle for liberation are a part of a renewing and renewable process. Hagar learns this after God sends her back to Sarah. The Hebrews find it when, after a spectacular escape from Egypt, they languish in the wilderness for a generation. In both cases, God introduces patience and faith into the liberation story. Thus, these two virtues accompany the working of God's justice in the world.

Rosa Parks had both. She complained about the segregated facilities for most of her adult life until she decided to do something about the situation. At that moment of destitution, she responded to God's call in the wilderness (of a segregated bus) and she cried out and God saw, heard, and delivered. Women receive these messages from the Hagar story. It is a story about a woman enslaved, pointing to a story about a people who will be enslaved. It is a story about a woman in the wilderness, pointing to a story about a people in the wilderness. It is a story about a woman who is blessed by God, pointing to a story about a people who will be blessed by God. Hagar's story is universal in that it is a story about God's work in the world to exact justice for the oppressed.

God exacts justice by giving sustenance and blessings in the wilderness. God did it for the Israelites. God did it for Jesus. And God did it for African American men and women. The justice that comes out of the wilderness experience of Hagar is not unlike the justice initiated by the actions of Rosa Parks to fight the oppression of blacks—actions that changed the status of blacks in the United States. Many other African American women have made justice a part of their ethics of black womanhood. They continue to be vocal advocates against unjust systems.

Justice Reading Strategy: Hagar, the Matriarch of the Arab Nation

Historical note: in the judgment of some historians, Abraham's migration into Canaan as portrayed in Genesis 12:1–6 was connected in some way with the Amorite infiltration into Mesopotamia and Syria. In this view, Abraham lived during the eighteenth century B.C.E. and may have been a contemporary of the Amorite king Hammurabi. Haran, Abraham's hometown, was an Amorite settlement in that period. The Amorite personal names, such as Benjamin (Binu-yamina), Jacob (Ya'qub-el), and Abram (Abamram), may not refer to the biblical characters themselves, but they certainly point to a common Semitic background.[11]

The story of Hagar does not end with the Hebrew Scriptures for the Islamic and Arab world. Hagar, as the mother of Ishmael, is considered to be the matriarch of the Arab people and the Islamic religion, and she is celebrated as such. Where the Hebrew text leaves Hagar in the wilderness, the Arab historical and sacred writings follow her through to her death and maintain her memory by honoring her as the matriarch of a nation. While some commentators on the Hebrew Scriptures speculate that there is more than one Hagar story (see the discussion in the section "The Two-Story Thesis"), the historians of the Qur'an and the history of the Arab people actually have various versions of the Hagar/Sarah/Abraham narrative.

This is evident in *The History of al-Tabari,* which is considered the "most important universal history produced in the world of Islam. It traces the stories of the factual and legendary accounts of ancient Iran, and details the rise of Islam and the life of the Prophet Mohammed."[12]

More important, for the purpose of this chapter, it also elaborates on the extrabiblical stories that intersect with the Hebrew Scriptures. Prominent among these narratives is the story of Abraham, Hagar, and Ishmael, the patriarch and matriarch of the Arab people. In providing another worldview of Hagar, it is important to recognize that when her plight is viewed in a different context, she embodies different characteristics emerging from a more positive ethos.

In documenting the history, al-Tabari refers to various versions of the story as told by different writers or as found in different oral traditions. This chapter summarizes some of the variations on the stories about Hagar, Abraham, Ishmael, Sarah, and Isaac. Many of the histori-

cal accounts predate Islam, which was founded around 700 C.E. With
the emergence of Islam, however, much in the manner of the redactors
of the Hebrew Scriptures, the Arab writers edited some of the older
writings to fit into contemporary cultural and religious traditions.

The narrative differs in many ways from the biblical story because it
serves as the foundation for the origin of the Islamic religion and the
parentage of the Arab race. Abraham, who is held in high regard by the
Islamic believers and is revered much the same as he is in the Hebrew
Scriptures, takes his wife, Sarah, to Egypt and passes her off as his sister.
Pharaoh, who takes her in to be his concubine, finds out that he has
been deceived, releases her, and gives her Hagar as a maidservant. Some
sources say that Hagar was Pharaoh's daughter; others, that she was a
slave girl. One refrain from a source repeats the phrase, "This is your
mother, O Arabs," after the mention of Hagar's name.[13]

The narrative continues: "[Sarah said,] 'I consider her a clean woman,
so take her. Perhaps God will grant you a son from her.' For Sarah was
barren and had grown old without bearing a son for Abraham. Abraham
had prayed to God to grant him a pious son, but the prayer was not answered until he had become old and Sarah barren. So he had intercourse
with Hagar, and she bore him Ishmael."[14]

According to this historical account, Abraham is said to have left
Egypt for Syria and settled in what is now Palestine with Sarah, Hagar,
and Ishmael. Considered one of the early pre-Islamic prophets,
Abraham establishes a place of worship in Syria before being called by
God to go to Mecca to build another house of worship for God.

The story follows along the line of the Hebrew text; the Abraham
story is interrupted by the destruction of what is called the "people of
Lot" (Sodom and Gomorrah), followed by the visit of the three mes-
sengers who tell Sarah that she will bear a child. Upon hearing this,
Abraham says: "Praise be to God who has granted me, despite my age,
Ishmael and Isaac. Verily my Lord is One Who hears prayer!"[15]

A messenger is then sent to Abraham (some say it was Gabriel, a
messenger from God), telling him to go and build a house for the worship of God. Abraham takes Hagar and Ishmael with him and goes to

the land of the present-day Mecca to build a place for worship. As Abraham leaves to build the house, he leaves Hagar and Ishmael behind without food or drink. Hagar speaks to him, saying, "O Abraham! To whom are you entrusting us?" He replies, "To God." She says, "Then go! He will not lead us astray."[16]

While Hagar and Ishmael wait for Abraham, they become thirsty, and Hagar climbs a mountain looking for water. As Hagar seeks water for Ishmael, an angel calls her, and here the dialogue departs even further from the Hebrew text: "Gabriel called out to her saying, 'Who are you?' She answered, 'Hagar, mother of the son of Abraham.' Gabriel said, 'To whom did he entrust you?' She said, 'He entrusted us to God.' He answered, 'He has entrusted you to One who is sufficient.'"[17]

When she returns to Ishmael, he has scraped the land and found water. There is a clear distinction between the Hagar of the Arab tradition and that of the Hebrew. She is empowered and liberated. Her identity as the mother of Ishmael is not one of shame, but one of pride. She responds to the question, "Who are you?" by claiming her parentage of Ishmael, not her position as a slave to Sarah. Clearly, this worldview allows for a more in-depth look at the character of Hagar.

The story goes on to reflect upon the conflict between Sarah and Hagar and introduces the custom of female circumcision. The custom is substantiated by a reference to a historical and religious act. Angry with Hagar, Sarah seizes her and performs the act on her.

When Isaac grew up, he and Ishmael fought. Sarah became angry and jealous toward Ishmael's mother and sent her away. Then she called her back and took her in. But later she became angry and sent her away again, and brought her back yet again. She swore to cut something off of her, and said to herself, "I shall cut off her nose, I shall cut off her ear—but no, that would deform her. I will circumcise her instead." So she did that, and Hagar took a piece of cloth to wipe the blood away. For that reason women have been circumcised and have taken pieces of cloth down to today.[18]

Unfortunately, the horrors of female circumcision are still prevalent today as a part of the religious and cultural practices of some Arabs, Africans, and Asians. Some critics feel that this religious-cultural integration of the custom is one of the impediments to the elimination of the practice.

From here on the story revolves around Abraham, Ishmael, and Hagar in the present-day Mecca, building a house for God. Upon Hagar's death, Ishmael takes a wife. Abraham does not approve of the first one; when Ishmael divorces or puts out the first one, Abraham visits and approves of the second. Consequently, there is a patriarchal remedy for the wife selection performed by Hagar in the Hebrew Scriptures. While there is no indication of who may have selected Ishmael's first wife, the authority to change wives is given to Abraham.

There are two statements to be made about the picture of Hagar that emerges from the history of the Arab peoples. The first is that she is not a slave with a slave's mentality. She is vibrant, faithful to God, and speaks frequently and forcefully. The second is that she is a formidable figure in the life of Abraham, a partner more than a concubine and a fellow traveler in the faith rather than an interloper with an alien faith and a different God.

From looking at this worldview of Hagar as an African woman in her own religious, cultural context, we may easily see how the Hebrew Scriptures could have evolved out of the stories of the Near Eastern cultures. On the other hand, if this is not the case, then we may see how the Arabs took the story of Hagar and crafted a foundation for a culture, a religion, and a nation.

For African American women, using the justice reading strategy allows them to remove Hagar from the box of oppression and place her in the context of a woman empowered by God to seek out creative ways to survive in times of need. Hagar climbs a mountain looking for water for her son. She does not resign herself to sitting under a tree waiting for her son to die. Oduyoye's point is well made in this respect. An African mother and an African American woman would indeed climb a mountain to save her child rather than retreat to a tree and watch him die.

Conclusion

This chapter has attempted to present the virtue of justice as seen in the narrative about Hagar and God. In looking at this virtue, it has also tied in as an exemplar of the beneficiary of justice, the mother of the civil rights movement, Rosa Parks. It was a movement based on the values of love and justice that was begun by the courageous act of a woman tired of injustice and determined to do something about it in a very ordinary circumstance. Parks set in motion the civil rights movement by taking a seat on the bus, initiating a movement that became the blueprint for transforming a society. Hagar set in motion a movement that became the blueprint for the biblical Exodus event. Each story speaks to God's ability to come into the world and transform the conditions of the oppressed by exacting justice through love. Chapter 3 offers reflection questions on Hagar and the virtue of justice.

Reflecting on Hagar

This chapter includes questions for reflection on the Hagar story as well as scriptures for biblical references to the virtue of justice. These questions can be used as a part of a group Bible study, or they can be used as an opportunity to grow in your personal spiritual development.

Reflections on Hagar and Justice

The following biblical references on justice can be used for further biblical reflection on justice as a virtue, justice as an attribute of God, and justice as a requirement for Christian community. They can be used as a means of personal ethical guidance and as a way to increase your understanding of the Bible.

   1. The following scriptures refer to justice as an attribute of God and as a prerequisite for community. Read them and reflect on your understanding of these scriptures in light of God's blueprint for justice as it appears in the Hagar narrative.

   Exodus 23:1–3, 6
   Leviticus 19:15

Deuteronomy 1:17
Deuteronomy 16:18–20
Isaiah 56:1
Isaiah 59:9
Jeremiah 23:5–6
Amos 5:21–24
Matthew 25:35–40

2. Other than God, the prophets represent the most consistent call for justice and righteousness. Read one of the following and reflect upon how this particular prophet petitioned for justice. Was it a plea to the people of Israel or on their behalf? How does each prophet define justice?

Isaiah 3:15
Jeremiah 22:3
Hosea 12:6
Amos 2:6–8
Amos 5:24
Micah 3:1–3

3. The following scriptures refer to God and justice, the nature of that justice, and the nature of God as a God who calls for "delivering the captives and setting at liberty those that are bound." Reflect upon how God exhibits impartial justice, especially as it relates to what the Bible considers to be foreigners in the midst of the chosen people. Does God dispense justice impartially to them? What is the most striking characteristic of God's justice, in your opinion?

Deuteronomy 32:4
Job 34:19
Psalm 11:7
Daniel 4:37
Romans 2:11
2 Thessalonians 1:6
1 Peter 2:23

4. When you think of the story of Hagar, can you relate any instance in your life or that of your family where destitution of a mother for a child led her to seek out God's face? Has this chapter sharpened your understanding of justice and given you some assurance of a just God in times of trouble?

5. How would you begin to develop a ministry that would establish a blueprint for exacting justice for mothers receiving welfare and families without homes? How would you see this materializing into a ministry for your church?

part two

L O V E

*If I speak in the tongues of mortals and of angels, but do not
have love, I am a noisy gong or a clanging cymbal. And if I have
prophetic powers, and understand all mysteries and all knowledge,
and if I have all faith, so as to remove mountains, but do not
have love, I am nothing. If I give away all my possessions, and
if I hand over my body so that I may boast, but do not have love,
I gain nothing.*

*Love is patient; love is kind; love is not envious or boastful
or arrogant or rude. It does not insist on its own way; it is not
irritable or resentful; it does not rejoice in wrongdoing, but rejoices
in the truth. It bears all things, believes all things, hopes all things,
endures all things. . . . And now faith, hope, and love abide,
these three; and the greatest of these is love. (1 Cor. 13:1–7, 13)*

Love as a Virtue and
Osceola McCarty

L ove is the core ethic of the gospel. It is the ethic that propels the acts of Jesus, forming the cornerstone of his gospel to a world in need of reconciliation and freedom from spiritual oppression. For Jesus, love is the one act that overcomes adversity and brings about a change in the condition of the oppressed, freeing their spirits so that they might participate in the reign of God.

The Latin terms *amor* and *caritas* and the principal Greek terms for love, *philia*, *eros*, and *agape*, provide a basis for the different dimensions of love that human beings express.

Philia refers to the kind of love involved in friendship; *amor* and *eros*, the type of love based on physical desires; and *caritas* and *agape* refer to a higher sense of calling—a selfless type of love. Thus, it is in the life of Jesus that agape love gains its deepest meaning as the unselfish love of humanity.

Using the eros/agape love distinction was popular during the civil rights movement. Popularizing the term *agape* was Dr. Martin Luther King Jr., who attempted to convey a more expansive vision of love for those who were suffering from the effects of segregation as well as for those who were perpetrating the wrongs against them. He went to great lengths to stress what was meant by agape love. For King and for other theologians, such as Howard Thurman, agape love forms the foundation of Christian ethics—the primary virtue to be embraced by all Christians.

King's theology of love was influenced in part by the works of the Swedish theologian Anders Nygren and the German-born theologian Paul Tillich. Nygren viewed the agape love of the Christian Scriptures as "the most powerful creative force in the universe. It is God's love for humanity. . . . Agape does not recognize value, but creates it. Agape love imparts value by loving. The man [or woman] who is loved by God has not value in himself [or herself]; what gives him [or her] value is precisely the fact that God loves him [or her]."[1]

Dr. King added another dimension to Nygren's love principle. In retrospective reflection, he labeled the civil rights movement a movement concerned not necessarily with nonviolence, but with Christian love. "It was the Sermon on the Mount, rather than a doctrine of passive resistance, that initially inspired the Negroes of Montgomery to dignified social action. It was Jesus of Nazareth that stirred the Negroes to protest with the creative weapon of love," wrote King.[2]

King went on to define Christian love not as sentimental love, but as "understanding, redemptive good will for all men (women). It is an overflowing love which is purely spontaneous, unmotivated, groundless, and creative. . . . Agape is disinterested love. It is a love in which the individual seeks not his own good, but the good of his neighbor (1 Cor. 10:24). . . . Agape is love seeking to preserve and create community."[3]

As a consequence of King's teachings on the now familiar distinction, the theme is often preached in Sunday morning worship services in churches around the country, but particularly in African American churches. Churches hold agape meals as a part of their ministries of reconciliation within and outside the church because it is believed that such meals, or "love feasts," were a significant part of the worship services of the early Christians.

Needless to say, agape love, when compared to eros and philia loves described and ascribed to by Aristotle and Plato, creates a different consciousness and a greater responsibility among people who embrace the love ethic as a virtue. Agape love surpasses human eros and philial loves and takes on a higher calling that promotes spiritual relationships among men and women, connectedness with God, and reconciliation with enemies. It is in the act of Jesus becoming human and sacrificing through human death on the cross that selfless love gains its ethos and credibility. As God demonstrated when moving from perfect being to imperfect man in the form of Jesus, this love that was freely given revolutionized the world.[4]

Martin Luther King Jr. talked often about this kind of love in his attempts to bring about a just society and a beloved community. Agape love, then, is the powerful dimension that speaks of sacrifice and unselfishness for the greater good of the human family. The list of African American women who have exemplified agape love is long—Sojourner Truth, Mary McLeod Bethune, Mother Hale, Harriet Tubman, Fannie Lou Hamer, and Mary Church Terrell, just to name a few. These names notwithstanding, a more recent story speaks to both the sacrifice and the love that Jesus teaches in the Scriptures.

Osceola McCarty

He sat down opposite the treasury, and watched the crowd putting money into the treasury. Many rich people put in large sums. A poor widow came and put in two small copper coins, which are worth a penny. Then he called his disciples and said to them, "Truly I tell you, this poor widow has put in more than all those who are contributing to the treasury. For all of them have contributed out of their abundance; but she out of her poverty has put in everything she had, all she had to live on." (Mark 12:41–44)

In 1995, the University of Southern Mississippi received a gift of $150,000 from an unlikely source. Maybe it was the memory of this scripture that caused the world to turn around and take notice of Osceola McCarty and her gift. Her contribution in dollars could easily have been dwarfed by most of the philanthropists and rich college alumni, but who she was and how she came about the money caused a cynical society to take time out to appreciate an unusual gift of love.

Perhaps it was an attempt to contribute to King's beloved community through an act of unselfishness and love that was brought to the attention of the public almost three decades after his death. In July 1995, four years before her death in September of 1999, Osceola McCarty, in the tradition of a long line of black women, displayed a bold act of agape love when the lifelong laundress gave $150,000 from her life's savings to the University of Southern Mississippi. McCarty had saved $280,000 over the course of her life as a domestic worker and felt that it was time to give a future generation an opportunity to go to college—a luxury she never enjoyed. Even though her gift was a small one compared to the millions that others give to universities, McCarty became a celebrity. Her celebrity status came not out of the amount of her gift, but out of the sacrifice and love that generated it. She commented,

> When I leave this world, I can't take nothing away from here. I'm old and I won't live always—that's why I gave the money to the school and put my affairs in order, I planned it and I am proud of it. I am proud that I worked hard and that my money will help young people who have worked hard to deserve it. I'm proud that I am leaving something positive in this world. My only regret is that I didn't have more to give.[5]

The octogenarian had never attended college, had never flown in an airplane, and had worked all her life in a domestic capacity as a laundress. However, following her act of love, Osceola McCarty found herself being honored at the White House by President William Clinton, speaking before television audiences as a guest on talk shows, being interviewed for newspapers and magazines, and being assigned her own collaborator for a book to write her life's story. It was an act of love so glaring in an uncaring world that it seemed that the world wanted to become a part of this one woman's gesture. Her gift captured the heart and imagination of the country because it was a symbol of love and sacrifice. These were virtues that the United States had forgotten about, but that McCarty took for granted. Infused in her ethic of womanhood were faith, love, sacrifice, and generosity. Her words now ring out from a book that captures the spirit behind her gift: "People ask me all the time who my friends are. I tell them that God is my best friend and that my mother was my next best friend. Them two loves you can't resist. . . . What I want people to know about Jesus is that there was nothing but love in Him. Even when they nailed his hands and feet he was loving. It helps to think about that when you are going through hard times."[6]

Osceola McCarty's story, much like the widow's offering in the parable, is a pristine example of agape love. It is clear to see the elements of love in the parable because of the simplicity of the story. There are no historical meanderings to determine why she did what she did or how she came to make this decision. No, it was just the nature of love as embodied in a woman who lived by her faith in God. Perhaps that is why Jesus chose the parable of the widow as a way of making the point about love—agape love that became the hallmark of the new covenant of God with humanity.

Osceola McCarty gave out of her love and sacrificed to give because of that love. It is a love that is deeper than eros or philia, more akin to the agape love of God who gave a son to save the world—a son who would in turn sacrifice his earthly life for humankind. As with the story of Osceola McCarty, this rich, deep, and abiding love can also be found in the story of Zipporah, the Midianite wife of Moses.

The Story of Zipporah: A Peculiar Woman in Salvation History

Scripture Readings

The following are biblical references to Zipporah. Read them before beginning this chapter.

- Moses rescues Zipporah and her sisters from a group of harassing shepherds. In turn, Reuel, her father, gives Zipporah to Moses in marriage. They marry and have a son, Gershom. (No mention is made in this passage to the birth of Eliezer; Exod. 2:16–22.)

- Zipporah circumcises her son and saves Moses' life (Exod. 4:24–26).

- Zipporah and her two sons are reunited with Moses in the wilderness (Exod. 18:2–6).

Introduction

In the creative and imaginative language of Zora Neale Hurston, the novelist and anthropologist, Zipporah is described as a woman with "tawny skin, night black eyes, red lips and crinkly hair." Although this image comes from Hurston's imagination, it provides a vivid picture of this first wife of Moses as a woman of color, substance, and attitude. It is here in her book *Moses, Man of the Mountain* that Hurston's view of Zipporah emerges. In Hurston's adaptation of the story, Zipporah and Moses were so much in love, he was unable to work without thinking about her. From this great African American novelist we get a picture of an African woman who loved and revered the Hebrew lawgiver and liberator.[1]

Hurston's view of the relationship between Moses and Zipporah was visually captured in 1998 when Hollywood produced an animated feature movie about Moses entitled *Prince of Egypt*.[2] In the Hollywood version, Zipporah was pictured as a spirited African woman devoted to Moses and his God-given mission.

The controversial production broke tradition by featuring animated Exodus characters as people of color. As could be expected, the production took some artistic liberties with the text as well. For example, Zipporah's first encounter with Moses takes place in the Egyptian palace where she is forcibly brought to dance and to be used as a sexual playmate for the young prince. She escapes this fate and flees as a wistful young Moses looks on. When he encounters her again, it is at the well where she is drawing water with her sisters. While Zipporah is introduced as a multidimensional woman with spirit and spunk, her role in the liberation mission of Moses is never brought to light in the movie. Thus, the most significant aspect of the text and of Zipporah's place in salvation history is omitted from this otherwise pioneering animated narrative.

From the African American pulpit comes another interpretation of Zipporah's relationship with Moses. In a sermon in his book *Africans Who Shaped Our Faith,* Rev. Jeremiah Wright, of Trinity United Church of Christ in Chicago, emphasizes Zipporah's role as the daughter of a priest and the wife of a preacher. Wright ascribes to her a spiritual wisdom and an attentiveness to ritual and tradition that form the foundation for her immediate response to Moses' attack by God. In the African American preaching tradition, Wright, with a dramatic style, contemporizes the story of Zipporah as he takes his unique liberty with the text. He paints a picture of a woman who is wise beyond her years, using the African rituals of her father to save the life of her husband.

These three portraits of Zipporah are far more generous than any of the traditional commentaries. Most do not acknowledge her role in salvation history at all. Still others are simply confused by the act of circumcision that she performs. In unraveling some of the mystery surrounding Zipporah, this chapter will retell the story, review her role in salvation history, and present an overview of traditional commentaries. Finally, this chapter will look at Zipporah's story using a justice reading strategy to give a global context to her place in God's plan for humanity. At the end of the chapter are reflection questions.

The Story

After killing an Egyptian and subsequently fleeing from Egypt, Moses found himself among the Midianites, a herding people of Hamitic descent. They were a powerful nomadic people who are said to have been the descendants of Keturah and Abraham with roots in Canaan, the Jordan Valley, Moab, and Transjordan (Gen. 25:1–2; 37:25–28; 36; 39:1; Exod. 2:15, 16, 21; Judg. 8:22–24; 1 Kings 11:18). One such group of the Midianites was believed to have been at one time a part of the Canaanite people, who fled following an attack on Canaan by the Hyksos. The Hyksos ruled Egypt and Canaan from around 1720 B.C.E. (the time of Abraham) to around 1700 B.C.E.[3]

According to one account:

> The Midianites established a black community that was as much as possible, economically independent of the Hyksos-controlled city-states—based on African values, run by a council of family elders. By the time the Midianites appear in scripture, they have become quite successful. By then, they are a large confederation of extended families located in Southeast Canaan, not far from

Mount Sinai. They have created at least two temples where the extended family members worshipped God.[4]

The stage is set, then, for Moses to be taken in by another African family and become a part of another African culture. While Moses is resting, the daughters of the Midianite priest Jethro (later called Reuel, "friend of God") attempt to dip water from a nearby well, but they are accosted by shepherds who begin to harass them. Moses chases the shepherds away and retrieves the water for the women, earning him an invitation to their tent. After hearing the story, Jethro rewards Moses by giving his eldest daughter, Zipporah, to him in marriage.

Moses and Zipporah marry and have the first of two sons, Gershom, whose name means "I am an alien there" (referring to Moses' life in either Midian or Egypt). Moses is later called by God to deliver the Israelites from bondage in Egypt.

When Moses responds to God's call, he brings along Zipporah and their two sons—Eliezer and Gershom. As they camp one night, an angel of God (or God) threatens to kill him. While the text gives no clue about why this encounter occurs, the swift action of Zipporah makes the difference in an otherwise unexplainable moment.

As a Midianite and the daughter of a priest, she knows that circumcision is an act of total commitment and total submission to God's will and way. She takes a flint and sharpens it, cuts the foreskin of her son, and puts it up to Moses' feet (some texts say genitals). Then she proclaims that he is "a bridegroom of blood" to her. This mysterious encounter ends, and God lets him go. This act seals the marriage between Moses and God. The circumcision and submission have taken place. "Now you are a bridegroom of blood by circumcision," Zipporah says (Exod. 4:26).

The ritual of conversion, the act of submission to God's will performed by Zipporah, stems from her love for Moses, for the people that he is to liberate, and for the God who called him. The act that Zipporah performs is referred to again when the Israelites first reach the promised land: "At that time God said to Joshua, 'Make flint knives and circumcise the Israelites a second time.' So Joshua made flint knives, and circumcised the Israelites at Gibeath-haaraloth" (Josh. 5:2–3).

Zipporah is mentioned again as Jethro takes her to Moses in the wilderness (Exod. 18:2–6). As he delivers Zipporah and her two sons, Jethro stays and gives Moses advice on how to manage the Israelites. Another reference to Zipporah may appear in Numbers 12:1–16 where Miriam criticizes Moses' "Cushite" wife. For doing this, she is cursed by God and afflicted with leprosy. Whether Miriam refers to Zipporah in her attack is not clear. This text assumes that it is not Zipporah, but another Cushite wife that Moses may have taken. Thus, this chapter reflects only upon the scripture readings that speak about Zipporah by name.

Zipporah's Role in Salvation History

Zipporah's overall significance becomes a lot clearer when using the justice reading strategy. In looking at the role of this African woman in the midst of her own culture, we see her actions and her role in the overall Hebrew story. Zipporah's story is worth telling because it has a direct impact on God's plan of salvation for the Hebrew people—she saves the life of their liberator. As a consequence, Moses, who owes his very life to women who acted swiftly and decisively to protect him from death, is once again put in a situation where a woman must ensure his survival.

In the past, there were women such as the midwives Shiphrah and Puah, who disobeyed the orders of Pharaoh and refused to kill the newborn Moses (Exod. 1:15–22); his mother, who took the decisive though painful action to put him in a basket to float to safety (Exod. 2:1–3); and his sister, Miriam, who was quick to suggest that a Hebrew woman (Moses' mother) should be hired to nurse him (Exod. 2:7–10), after Pharaoh's daughter made the decision to rear him as her own (Exod. 2:5–6).

Thus, Moses, the main character in the Hebrew story, is surrounded by women who engage in significant acts in the Hebrew salvation story but who traditionally have been treated as incidental to the narrative or unimportant to the overall work of God in history. While some may look at the Bible and lodge these critiques, the use of the justice reading strategy prevents them from coming to a conclusion that minimizes the role of these women. These acts are not incidental to the narrative, but prove to be of significance to the overall story of God's work in human history. Consequently, if women saved Moses' life five times, two things are important to mention: the first is that their role is not a marginalized one, and the second is that they are significant contributors to the fulfillment of God's plan for salvation. There is no question but that Zipporah changed the course of Moses' journey by acting out of love and spiritual knowledge to save his life.

Traditional Commentaries

Zipporah, however, has not fared very well in the hands of scholars and commentators on the Hebrew Bible. The more artistic and Africentric views of Zipporah are nowhere to be found in the scholarly commentaries on the first wife of Moses. Although Zipporah appears briefly in the Hebrew text, the act that she performs as Moses is en route to freeing the Israelites continues to perplex scholars. While most agree that their understanding of the symbolism of her decisive act of circumcising her son is limited, they nevertheless ascribe motives to her actions. Most consider it an act done not out of love, but out of frustration or malice. For example, one commentator writes:

> It is clear that either in deference to the wishes of Zipporah, or for some other reason, he failed to comply with the initial rite which had been enjoined on Abraham as the sign and seal of the covenant. . . . If God remembered the covenant, it was surely necessary that His servant should; and if the covenant was the basis of His interposition, it was imperative that the whole congregation should stand true to its obligations as well as its privileges. A sharp illness that smote Moses in the Khan seems to have reminded his wife as well as himself of this neglected rite; and Zipporah with an ill-grace yielded beneath the stern pressure of the hour. Probably she had been the stumbling-block, and now only gave way because she must. So her husband's life was spared. . . . It was clear that Zipporah would be of no real help to him in the difficult and perilous enterprise on which he

was engaging; and Moses appeared to have renounced his intention of taking her.[5]

Others have speculated that this act of circumcision and Moses' encounter with the angel of God resulted from his disobedience and his acquiescence to the customs of his wife, whose matriarchal society had placed her in charge of the children and whose decision had prevented their younger son, Eliezer, from being circumcised. The following quote is typical of this kind of commentary:

> Some tribes, especially in Arabia, had the custom of circumcising their young men prior to marriage. Moses, who was circumcised as a child, had now according to Zipporah, become her bridegroom after and because of circumcision, but the circumcision was that of her son. The word used here for "bridegroom" is related to an Arabic word meaning to "circumcise." Although I do not believe that Moses' marriage was originally matriarchal in nature (i.e., the woman considered the children to belong to her tribe since she continued living with her relatives and her husband moved in with her) and underwent a change here, it is true that during his journey to Egypt Moses emerged fully as the head of his household.
>
> This view gives the story the purpose of showing that Moses, before he could act as a leader and redeemer of Israel, was himself called to uphold the demands of the Lord as the God of the covenant.[6]

It is clear from these commentaries that many of the traditional approaches to this text not only carry undesirable patriarchal rationale, but also produce very little fruit. A new reading strategy is necessary if the scripture is to be given credibility and the story of Zipporah is to be given a place in God's salvation plan.

Justice Reading Strategy

Zipporah was a Midianite, a descendant of Abraham by his wife, Keturah (Gen. 25:1–4), and she was the first wife of Moses, given to him by her father, Jethro (Reuel), a Midianite priest. For Moses, marrying into the Midianite clan would provide him with a livelihood as a shepherd, a close-knit family, and a spiritual reference point for his own encounter with God. With advice from Jethro, Moses was able to transform an unruly band of ex-slaves into a loosely organized group of people able to respond to his leadership. This was done when Jethro reunited Moses with Zipporah and their two sons following the Exodus out of Egypt (Exod. 18:1–27). Every indication is that Jethro was a wise and spiritual man who believed in a monotheistic God and whose beliefs were shared by his eldest daughter, Zipporah.

The Midianites, a former Canaanite tribe, were shepherds and metallurgists who may have practiced an African monotheistic religion, of which Jethro was a priest:

> As a Cushite, it is possible that Jethro came from a line of priests who brought the African priesthood into the Midianite family network with them. . . . There is archaeological evidence that perhaps Jethro began as a traditional African priest, perhaps even as a part of the Egyptian Mystery System. Archaeological evidence suggests that the Midianite league of cities was grouped around a common shrine where the interconnected extended families worshipped and brought sacrifices.[7]

A portrait of Jethro, Zipporah's father, is much easier to paint than one of Zipporah. She appears in the text briefly and says a few, heretofore unexplainable, words. Scholars have puzzled over this difficult text. The questions raised are many: Why was God trying to kill Moses after commanding him to confront Pharaoh? Why was his life in danger? As previously mentioned, some commentators believe that his life was in danger because he had not circumcised his son as God required. Others have noted that it could be the case that he was not circumcised. One explanation could be that Zipporah, having been raised in a Near Eastern culture where circumcision was a ritual connoting commitment to God, performed the act in order to complete Moses' conversion to God. In so doing, she showed her love for the life of her husband (eros) and her love for his people (philial), and she risked the life of her son to protect Moses so that he might do the work of God (agape).

This latter explanation can be validated by looking at the story itself. Moses knew nothing about God. He asked God for a name because he knew no name. Zipporah, on the other hand, grew up in the household of a priest. As the eldest daughter, she was knowledgeable about his practices, rituals, and beliefs. It stands to reason that Zipporah provided a spiritual grounding for Moses, who was alienated from his own culture early in life and reared by the Egyptians.

Symbolically, Zipporah's act could have been looked upon as a prophetic act predating the actual second circumcision that would mark the entrance of the Hebrew people into the promised land. Even if this were the case, it does not remove the fact that Zipporah performed an act of love both for her husband and for God. Thus, Zipporah brings a cultural and religious rite into the salvation story, demonstrating once again that God had been "God" long before the Hebrew story unfolded. As other cultures move in and out of the story of the Hebrew people, they expand the understanding of the overall meaning of salvation and God's plan for an inclusive humanity.

Conclusion

Zipporah's role in God's salvation story is often underrepresented, if not forgotten. She saves Moses from death and prepares him for the spiritual and physical liberation of the Hebrew people, whose story the Bible celebrates. Out of the eros love and the philial love comes the agape love that is celebrated as one of the central biblical virtues. As in his infancy, Moses is again saved by a woman of African descent, enabling him to fulfill the plan that God has for his life. Although commentators usually have a different worldview and either dismiss this text or express a sense of confusion about how it came about, a justice reading strategy makes it clear that without the Africanism brought to the fore by Zipporah, Moses' mission would not have been accomplished. God interceded at this point and made Zipporah the vehicle for dispensing much-needed wisdom and insight.

As for Zipporah's attitude toward performing the circumcision, again, the commentators, primarily male and Western, lose sight of the relationship that existed between the two. While any comment on this relationship is speculative, this reading of the events produces another vision of Zipporah, the wife of Moses. It envisions an African woman whose husband is about to embark on a major journey—a spiritual journey—headed to tell the most powerful man in the ancient world to free his people. Moses, unsure and insecure, brings along his strong and spiritual wife, Zipporah, the daughter of a priest who is knowledgeable about the rituals and rites of religion. Zipporah's role is more significant when looking at Moses' history with God. Moses is a reluctant deliverer and a person who did not know who God was, nor did he know what name to call God. Since circumcision became a religious rite among the Hebrews after they borrowed the practice from the Egyptians and the religions of other Near Eastern peoples, it is not clear how much Moses knew about the ritual at all.

Zipporah knew about the circumcision covenant, and when she witnessed that Moses angered God, she knew what to do immediately. Prescient and wise, this daughter of a priest had courage. It was courage born out of her love for her husband, but also from her love for God. Zipporah took a flint, much as Joshua would later do at the command of God, and cut off the foreskin of her son and touched Moses' feet with it. It was an act of deep love, not contempt. Zipporah knew that Moses had been chosen for a mighty work. Her part was a small one, but she played it well. God was testing Moses. Moses needed to make the final commitment through the covenant of blood.

Zipporah, the Midianite, knew that Moses, unsure, needing assurance, was still hesitant. God needed someone with courage. Moses needed to be tough. Aristotle stated that wisdom precedes courage. Zipporah was both courageous and wise. It was love that made her do it. Agape love.

Reflecting on Zipporah

This chapter includes questions for reflection on the story of Zipporah as well as scriptural references for biblical reflection on the virtue of love. These questions can be used as part of a group Bible study, or they can be used as part of a personal spiritual growth and development discipline.

Reflections on Zipporah and Love

The following biblical references to love can be used for further biblical reflection on love as a virtue, love as an attribute of God, and love as a requirement for Christian community. These scriptures can be used as a means of personal spiritual growth and development and as a way of increasing your understanding of the Bible.

1. The following passages reflect on human love for God and for one another:

Matthew 10:37
John 8:42
John 13:34–35

John 15:12, 17
1 John 4:21

2. The following passages reflect on God's love for us:

John 16:27
Romans 1:7
2 Thessalonians 2:16
Titus 3:4–5
1 John 4:8, 16

3. When you reflect on the story of Zipporah, how do you interpret her actions, and what do you believe God is saying to us in this story?

4. Love is a peculiar emotion. How have you experienced love in your life, and what do you consider to be the most profound feeling of love that you have experienced? How would you compare it with the love of God?

5. Not everyone gives love freely. What do you believe to be some of the barriers to expressing love freely? Is this a question that Christians should ask themselves as they grow closer to Christ?

part three

FAITH

*Now faith is the assurance of things hoped for, the conviction
of things not seen. Indeed, by faith our ancestors received approval.
By faith we understand that the worlds were prepared by
the word of God, so that what is seen was made from things
that are not visible. (Heb. 11:1–3)*

Faith as a Virtue and Sojourner Truth

Faith is the invisible bond that binds together the human family with the divine purpose of God. It is the foundation of the Christian witness and the precondition for hope. Faith kept African American women strong against all odds, and faith kept them from losing hope in the midst of despair.

Faith kept Harriet Tubman going back for more slaves, faith kept Sojourner Truth speaking out against slavery, faith made Ida B. Wells Barnett believe that she could change a country's lynching laws, and faith kept countless unnamed mothers moving from one day to the next, not knowing what the future held for them or their families.

From the Latin *fidere* (to trust), faith is defined as an attitude or belief that goes beyond the available evidence. There are both religious and nonreligious forms of faith. This chapter will discuss religious faith only, as found in the Hebrew Scriptures and the Christian Scriptures.

One of the classic debates in theology centers on the role of faith in salvation. Is it faith alone or faith and works that lead to salvation? The two scriptural sources most frequently referred to in this debate emerge from the writings of Paul and those found in James. The apostle Paul, announcing the end of the era of Mosaic law, held that justification was henceforth to be by faith, not works. The writer of James, on the other hand, declared that faith without works is dead. As evidence of that position, he gave the example of Rahab, the prostitute in Jericho, who hid the Israelite spies, in addition to acknowledging the power of God, in exchange for the safety and lives of her family members. Whether we are justified by faith alone, or by faith and works as evidenced by Rahab, is not a question that will be debated in this book. It is necessary, however, to raise the issue to give context to the various understandings of faith in the life of believers.

The unique concept of religious faith has also been debated by philosophers, who have always been confounded by religious faith because it does not require proof to exist. Faith can be explicit, implicit, or infused. When faith is explicit, it is said that a person agrees to a truth without complete knowledge of the facts. Faith is said to be implicit when there is no knowledge of the truth, but belief is still present. Faith is said to be infused when there is no explanation within the human realm of understanding.[1]

The Bible discusses faith as a virtue in passages such as 1 Corinthians 13:2, 13; Hebrews 11; and 1 Timothy 6:1–10. The biblical call is for believers to cultivate faith through trials and tribulations as a way to build character, endurance, and a more perfect relationship with God: "My brothers and sisters, whenever you face trials of any kind, consider it nothing but joy, because you know that the testing of your faith produces endurance; and let endurance have its full effect, so that you may be mature and complete, lacking in nothing" (James 1:2–4).

Many African American women have had to endure the vicissitudes of life and have come to the conclusion that their travails were made all the more bearable because they knew of the assurance of God's grace. This endurance made them better persons in Christ, and their faith gave them a cushion that softened the blows of life's heavy burdens. They believed literally in taking their burdens to God and leaving them there.

"Discipline yourselves, keep alert. Like a roaring lion your adversary the devil prowls around, looking for someone to devour. Resist him, steadfast in your faith, for you know that your brothers and sisters in all the world are undergoing the same kinds of suffering. And after you have suffered for a little while, the God of all grace, who has called you to eternal glory in Christ, will restore, support, strengthen, and establish you" (1 Peter 5:8–10).

The Bible also offers examples of the faithful. The writer of Hebrews 11:4–39 recalls the faith stories of Abel, Enoch, Noah, Abraham, and Moses as well as Gideon, Barak, Samson, Jephthah, and David. Hebrews, of course, compares all of these faithful lives to that of Jesus: "Therefore, since we are surrounded by so great a cloud of witnesses, let us also lay aside every weight and the sin that clings so closely, and let us run with perseverance the race that is set before us, looking to Jesus the pioneer and perfecter of our faith, who for the sake of the joy that was set before him endured the cross, disregarding its shame, and has taken his seat at the right hand of the throne of God" (Heb. 12:1–2). Thus, faith as a Christian virtue is regarded as a high calling because the life of Jesus is its exemplar.

When we look at the long line of African American women who could stand in the gap to represent faith, one woman's story comes to mind; it is that of Sojourner Truth. On June 1, 1843, Pentecost Sunday, Isabella Van Wagenen changed her name to Sojourner Truth and headed east to "where the spirit called her" to preach the gospel. After changing her name, this stalwart woman from New York began creating a life that explored the vibrant religious movements of her day. On the eve of the Second Great Awakening, Sojourner Truth experienced this conversion and joined the Methodist movement that was burgeoning in the early 1800s.[2]

Preaching at the outdoor meetings and joining in the communities of faith, living in integrated communes in the North, Truth was known among her contemporaries more for her evangelical appeal than her alleged legendary involvement in the suffrage and abolitionist movements. The most recent unmasking of her role in the Second Great Awakening came as a result of a book by Nell Painter entitled *Sojourner Truth: A Life, a Symbol,* in which she dispelled some of the myths surrounding the level of Truth's involvement in the women's suffrage movement.

More than anything else, Sojourner Truth was a woman of faith and action. She joined a society that helped prostitutes get out of the streets, the Magdalene Society, and there became a voice and an advocate for the evangelical movements of the 1800s. After her involvement with a number of charismatic religious movements, Sojourner Truth (itinerant preacher) began preaching the gospel wherever she traveled. In the late 1800s, Truth once again joined a religious community, this time the Northhampton Association in Massachusetts.[3]

The extent of Sojourner Truth's faith journey through a period of time in the United States when spiritual awakening was pervasive is little known. Her constant search for an ideal community of faith took Truth from communes to utopian societies as she tried to live out the Christian life. Her deep commitment to the application of her faith to justice became the hallmark of her life and work. A gifted preacher and an evangelist, Truth was lauded for bringing these gifts to aid the causes of freedom, abolition, and women's rights. While not the most significant part of her life, these areas nevertheless became her historic recorded contributions. But even in these, she brought her spiritual convictions and her deep commitment to Christianity.

As an antislavery lecturer, she uttered her first famous phrase in the late 1840s as Frederick Douglass was doubting the possibility of ending slavery peaceably: "Frederick, is God dead?" This rhetorical question established her as a Christian of exquisite faith in accordance with nineteenth-century evangelical sensibilities. But this phrase's popularity had begun to fade by the century's end. Modern audiences are more likely to know Truth as a feminist who redefines womanhood along very contemporary lines.[4]

Thus, the faith and Christian consciousness of Sojourner Truth are hidden in the history that extols her virtues as being a part of a worldly battle for justice, but the impetus that transformed Sojourner Truth from the slave girl Isabella came from her commitment to God, not her commitment to an earth-bound political cause, such as the suffrage movement. Her work with prostitutes was more representative of her social justice consciousness.

Rahab, a woman of faith, is also one who is better known for the work that she performed rather than for the faith that she exhibited. Known as Rahab the prostitute, this Canaanite woman had more than just a past profession that could have defined her; she put her faith to the test for the sake of her family and herself. Like Sojourner Truth, she was a peculiar woman of faith, not defined by the world but defined by her relationship with God.

The Story of Rahab: From Prostitute to Ancestor of Jesus

Scripture Readings

The following are biblical references to Rahab. Read them before beginning this chapter.

- Rahab takes in the Israelite spies, acknowledges the power of God, and bargains for her life and the lives of her family members (Josh. 2:1–20).
- Joshua announces that Rahab's house will be spared because she saved the spies (Josh. 6:17).
- Rahab and her family are saved as the Israelites take Jericho (Josh. 6:23–25).
- Rahab is listed as a spiritual ancestor of Jesus (Matt. 1:5).
- Rahab is mentioned as an example of the faithful (Heb. 11:31).
- Rahab is put forth as an example of faith with works (James 2:25).

Introduction

The story of Rahab calls for weighing virtues against the cause of right and wrong. Rahab was a prostitute, a woman whose very lifestyle is cause for ethical concern. She lived on the outskirts of Canaan near the Jericho wall, a virtual outcast from society. Her lifestyle afforded her many liberties and responsibilities that other women did not have; she was the economic resource for her family and apparently their protector in many ways. Even if she can be forgiven for this lifestyle, her manipulation of the situation with the spies is questionable.

Rahab's story, then, forces the reader to look at the issue of ethics in a broader sense. What are the overriding criteria for determining which of her actions should be celebrated and which should be condemned? This woman, whose lifestyle was already a questionable one, further complicated her moral standing by becoming a traitor to her people in order to save herself and her family.

Hers is indeed a peculiar faith journey, and it begs the question: Can anything good come out of this story? This chapter will attempt to shed some light on the many levels of interpretation of this story about this African woman's faith journey.

The Story

As Joshua attempts to conquer the land of Canaan, he sends spies into Jericho to report on what is happening in the town and to get a lay of the land before the Israelites move in on them. The two spies enter the town, come to the house of Rahab, a prostitute, and spend the night there. When the king finds out, he commands Rahab to bring the men out, but she hides them instead and reports to the king that they have left the house and that she has no knowledge of where they may have gone. In the meantime, as the king's men pursue the spies, Rahab goes up to the roof and begins bargaining with the spies. She explains to them that she has heard about the power of their God and that it has caused the people of Jericho to fear God.

Rahab successfully bargains for the lives of her mother and father and sisters and brothers and herself. The men agree that as long as she remains silent about their plans, they will honor their commitment to spare her family. Once she lets them down from the roof and gives them instructions on how to evade the king's men, they then put a condition on her request for safety. The spies tell her to put a crimson cord in the window.

The spies go back and report what Rahab has said about the land being theirs and the people fearing them. This report comes not from their own surveillance but from the words of Rahab. In Joshua 6:23–25, Joshua delivers on the promise to save the house of Rahab.

Rahab is mentioned in three books of the Christian Scriptures. The first mention is in Matthew 1:5, where the writer notes that she is one of the spiritual ancestors of Jesus. The next mention is in Hebrews, where she is identified with Moses and others as one of the faithful. In James her actions are used to prove that "faith without works is dead."

Thus, throughout the text, her faith changes her condition—from a prostitute outside society to an ancestor of Jesus inside the story of salvation. Consequently, this African woman is an integral part of the salvation story. The remainder of the chapter will feature the traditional interpretations of the story and a justice reading strategy for the story. Chapter 9 offers reflection questions about her story.

Traditional Commentary

Many scholars and theologians have looked at the story of Rahab and have provided interpretations on various levels. For example, John Calvin deals with the ethics of her actions and what constitutes the greater good:

> Now the questions which here arise are, first, was treachery to her country excusable? Secondly, could her lie be free from fault? We know that the love of our country, which is as it were our common mother, has been implanted in us by nature. When, therefore, Rahab knew that the object intended was the overthrow of the city in which she had been born and brought up, it seems a detestable act of inhumanity to give her aid and counsel to the spies. It is a puerile evasion to say, that they were not yet avowed enemies, inasmuch as war had not been declared;

since it is plain enough that they had conspired the destruction of her fellow citizens. It was therefore only the knowledge communicated to her mind by God which exempted her from fault as having been set free from the common rule. Her faith is commended by two Apostles, who at the same time declare (Heb. xi.31; James ii.25) that the service which she rendered to the spies was acceptable to God.

Is it not wonderful, then, that when the Lord condescended to transfer a foreign female to his people, and to ingraft her into the body of the Church, he separated her from a profane and accursed nation. Therefore, although she had been bound to her country men up to that very day, yet when she was adopted into the body of the Church, her new condition was a kind of manumission from the common law by which citizens are bound toward each other. In short, in order to pass by faith to a new people, she behoved to renounce her countrymen. And as in this she only acquiesced in the judgment of God, there was no criminality in abandoning them.[1]

Calvin's concern about Rahab is tempered in the end by the appearance of her name in the long line of genealogy that Matthew uses to legitimate Jesus' divine and human nature. Rahab is listed along with three other women, who also are Gentiles and/or, like Mary, had unique personal histories—Ruth, a widow and Moabitess; Bathsheba, the Hittite and adulteress; and Tamar, the Canaanite who posed as a prostitute and was impregnated by Judah, her father-in-law. They have all come together now as ancestors of Jesus. Lauded for her faith, Rahab also exhibited resourcefulness and in the final analysis a form of justice that made way for the chosen people of God to inhabit the land promised to them by God.

Other commentators have looked at the story from different vantage points. One analysis breaks up the story into three parts. In the first two parts, the spies are caught in the trap of Rahab, and Rahab sets forth stipulations while they are entrapped. In the third part, the spies escape from the trap and renegotiate the conditions with Rahab. In this com-

mentary, Rahab is seen to be in control of the first two parts, and the
spies, once they get outside her house, are in control of the last part
where the stipulation is changed to require Rahab to hang out the crimson cord in order to be saved. The same commentator evaluates the
manner in which Rahab stands in the middle of the success or failure of
Joshua or the king. Rahab's decision to lie to the king's men makes it
possible for Joshua to gain victory over them.[2]

Rahab is no doubt a manipulator and a negotiator. Weighing the
odds of the victory, she has chosen to take the side of the Israelites because she has heard that their God is victorious. This survival instinct—
more than faith in the God of Israel—appears to motivate her to act
against her country and for the insurgent Israelites. This certainly explains her actions, but what explains her movement from prostitute to
paragon of faith, justice, and courage? The answer can be found in looking at Rahab's role in God's plan for salvation. Rahab, the Canaanite
woman, can legitimately be considered a significant player in God's divine plan for humanity.

The basic premise of this commentary is that Rahab was interjected
into a story about spying and the strategies used for the Hebrews to conquer Canaan. In other words, she was just placed in the story as a literary foil for the purpose of describing the spying strategy. Obviously, if
this line of reasoning is followed, there is no theological or spiritual basis
for Rahab's appearance in the text. The commentator goes on to dis-
credit the emphasis on Rahab:

> The plot interest centers on how Rahab safeguards them and in
> the process extracts an important concession to rescue herself
> and her family. Here we can recognize a typical ethnological saga
> in which a wily ancestor helps herself and her kinfolk through
> shrewdness and presence of mind. She does so by shielding im-
> periled visitors and forcing from them a promise of future pro-
> tection. Rahab is a trickster. She seems to help the king, but
> tricks him. She seems to aid the spies, but traps them. At this
> level the saga provides an etiology for the continued existence of
> a non-Israelite group, the house of Rahab in or near Jericho

(Joshua 6:25). . . . Although the continued existence of Rahab's clan may not have been too pressing a concern for greater Israel, the larger issue of the presence of alien peoples would remain important into the monarchy and long afterward.[3]

Clearly, in this commentary, there is no room for a perspective of Rahab that would allow her to be a legitimate part of the salvation plan of God. She is considered an incidental character whose role is to justify why the Hebrews did not commit total genocide on the Canaanites. Yet this does not account for the reason why she is included in Matthew's genealogy of Jesus.

Other comments have alluded to the sexual innuendoes in the text and the writing. The language used by the spies, which could imply intercourse (Gen. 19:33, 35), and the king's exchange with Rahab, which they consider ambiguous (Josh. 2:3–4) and laced with sexual connotations, are used as ways to denigrate the spiritual aspects of the story and point to the oft-repeated criticism of the Canaanites as cultist people with sexual rituals accompanying their worship of Baal, their god. Even Rahab's name, which means "wide," alludes to sexual overtones for the story.[4]

All of these commentaries would place the role of Rahab below the threshold of God's grace and into a position where she is not considered worthy of being blessed by God through this encounter. The justice reading strategy offers another approach.

Justice Reading Strategy

The story of the Hebrew people's conquest of Canaan is generally the overriding concern of the writers and commentators who speak to the spiritual history of the people of Israel. Granted, the Hebrew text rewrites the history of this people as a people favored by God. However, the Rahab story, the story of the first convert to God in the promised land, focuses the attention on this woman of color who will also partake in the promised land blessing. Not only does she enable the Hebrews to fulfill the promise of God; she also represents the manner in which God will work in the promised land to include others in the blessing.

Some historical extrabiblical commentaries identify Rahab as the wife of Joshua. There is no way to tell whether that interpretation is correct, but Rahab undoubtedly was a significant presence in the history of the Hebrew people because she appears in the spiritual lineage of Jesus. Such an appearance speaks to her historical and religious role in the salvation story. With the justice reading strategy, it is possible to look at the message that can be derived from this story. Belief in God distinguished the people who benefited from the promised land blessing, which included not only those who had been delivered from slavery in Egypt, but all who acknowledged Yahweh as God. Thus, in the promised land, belief in Yahweh, not being Hebrew, made the people of Israel special. It was their faith, not their ethnicity, that was important to their covenantal relationship with God. Rahab's example of her faith provides that first lesson. By her actions and her faith, she becomes a part of the divine plan of salvation. A compassionate God looked with favor on an "outsider" who, through her faith and belief, risked everything in order to become a part of the promised land experience. This is the nature and the call of the faith of Rahab, a Canaanite, who believed in Yahweh.

9

Reflecting on Rahab

This chapter includes questions for reflection on the Rahab narrative as well as scriptural references about the virtue of faith. These questions can be used as a part of a group Bible study, or they can be used as an opportunity to grow in personal spiritual development.

Reflections on Rahab and Faith

The following biblical references on faith can be used for further biblical reflection on faith as a virtue and as a requirement for Christian community. These passages can be used as a means of personal ethical guidance and as a way of increasing your understanding of the Bible.

1. The following passages are only a few of those that refer to faith as a virtue. Read them and reflect on your understanding of them in light of God's call for you to be faithful.

   2 Corinthians 4:16–18
   Ephesians 6:10–20
   1 Timothy 6:11–16

Hebrews 11:1–3
James 5:13–20

2. Rahab not only professed her faith, but she also matched it with her works. What is your theology? Do you believe that we are saved by faith alone, or by faith and works? What scriptural references do you use to support your belief?

3. Why do you believe that Rahab is included in the spiritual ancestry of Jesus? Why do you believe the other women—Bathsheba, Ruth, Tamar, and Mary—are included?

4. What is your view of Rahab? Do you believe that there was any justification for her lying to the king about the spies? Do you believe that she did it for the sake of God's plan for salvation or for the sake of saving her own life?

5. Do you know any prostitutes? How would you use this scripture to get them to think about changing their lives? Would you be willing to go out and teach this story to women who have lost their self-esteem or who are exploited by men and used as prostitutes?

part four

WISDOM

Wisdom teaches her children
*   and gives help to those who seek her.*
Whoever loves her loves life,
*   and those who seek her from early morning are filled with joy.*
Whoever holds her fast inherits glory
*   and God blesses the place she enters.*
Those who serve her minister to the Holy One;
*   God loves those who love her.*
Those who obey her will judge the nations,
*   and all who listen to her will live secure.*
If they remain faithful, they will inherit her;
*   their descendants will also obtain her. (Sirach 4:11–16)*

Wisdom as a Virtue and Mary McLeod Bethune

What is wisdom, and why is it an important virtue? While secular definitions of wisdom usually define it as an application of "comprehensive knowledge," the biblical definition generally includes a relationship with God as one of its major criteria.[1] Usually personified as a woman, wisdom is used in the Bible in two contexts, human and divine.

In the former [human wisdom], it has a wide range of meanings: human skill, practical knowledge, magic, ability to coin wise sayings, and meditation on the Law. In the latter, it refers to the infinite wisdom of God in creation and in the guidance of the destinies of peoples and nations. In the later Old Testament period, there was a tendency to talk of this wisdom as if it were independently real, a tendency which made it natural for later Christian theologians to identify wisdom with the logos or second person of the Trinity. This was facilitated by St. Paul's assertion that Jesus "is the wisdom of God" (1 Corinthians 1:24), and the Johannine claim that Jesus Christ is the embodiment of the eternal Logos which was in the beginning with God and was God (John 1:1–16).[2]

Probably the most famous scripture concerning wisdom is the prayer of Solomon while on top of Mount Gibeon (1 Kings 3:1–15; 2 Chron. 1:2–13). Recognizing that he had a tremendous task ahead as king of Israel, the young Solomon asked God for an understanding mind/heart[3] to govern the people and to be able to discern good from evil. God not only responded with the gift of wisdom for Solomon but also gave him wealth, for which he did not ask. Solomon wanted to be able to dispense justice with the knowledge that he gained and with the guidance of God so that his decisions would be blessed and correct.

Solomon's example points to the most important element in the Hebrew Scriptures' definition of wisdom—it is a dynamic relationship between God and men and women that results in a unique process for distinguishing between right and wrong as well as between wise action and foolishness. Wisdom is not intelligence, knowledge, or individual decision making; rather, it is a religious encounter between the human and the Divine. The theological ingredient in wisdom that makes it a special virtue is its dependence upon God as a significant element in the discernment process. Knowledge alone does not produce wisdom. For Solomon, gaining wisdom was a part of his covenant with God, and it was affirmed to the world outside Israel by the words and the visit of the Queen of Sheba (1 Kings 10:1–10, 13). The queen marveled not only at Solomon's wisdom, but also at the God of Israel who gave it to him and placed him on the throne to rule the Hebrews.

In the Gospels, wisdom became the province of Jesus. Jesus was the embodiment of wisdom and the cause for confounding those who were usually considered wise. As Paul wrote in 1 Corinthians 1:20–25:

Where is the one who is wise? Where is the scribe? Where is the debater of this age? Has not God made foolish the wisdom of the world? For since, in the wisdom of God, the world did not know God through wisdom, God decided, through the foolishness of our proclamation, to save those who believe. For Jews demand signs and Greeks desire wisdom, but we proclaim Christ crucified, a stumbling block to Jews and foolishness to Gentiles, but to those who are the called, both Jews and Greeks, Christ the power of God and the wisdom of God. For God's foolishness is wiser than human wisdom, and God's weakness is stronger than human strength.

Wisdom, then, is a vital element in the biblical writings and in the gospel story, so much so that Jesus is considered to be God's wisdom on earth. To further understand the importance of wisdom in the Hebrew culture and the cultures that surrounded Israel, we need only to look at the writings in Psalms, Proverbs, Ecclesiastes, Job, and the Song of Solomon, as well as Sirach and the Wisdom of Solomon in the Apocrypha. These books, known as wisdom literature, are a combination of biblical references to wisdom and borrowings from the Near Eastern cultures that surrounded Israel. "Wisdom was not only a class of writings in ancient Israel; it was first and foremost a way of life and of understanding the world. The wise man or sage was one who sought to look deeply into the meaning of things, and as such he was a valued member of society. He was associated with various (related) professions: royal counselor and court adviser, judge, teacher, scribe."[4]

Outside these books are other references within the various stories of the Bible that talk about wisdom, or in which songs or oracles are given that result from the prophets or others who are said to embody wisdom. By and large, the Bible engages in gender-free narratives when speaking of wisdom. But when wisdom is personified, it is usually personified as a woman. A number of women in Scripture, including Deborah, the prophetess (Judg. 4:4–24), and the "wise woman" of Tekoa (2 Sam. 14:1–20) give wise counsel to men.

It is easy to see how African American women in their quest to redefine womanhood would choose wisdom as one of the virtues that built character and helped formulate their concept of the virtuous black woman. For African American women, the combination of knowledge, intuition, and spiritual guidance produced a legacy of women who were considered wise. They included the unlearned as well as the learned. They included the recorded heroines as well as the unrecorded ones. They were grandmothers, aunts, and mothers who gave valuable advice about life based on their experience seen through the prism of their faith. One of the most noted was Mary McLeod Bethune, an educator, an advisor to presidents, and a woman committed to the uplift of black women and their families.

Wisdom is what Mary McLeod Bethune exhibited as she turned a $1.50 investment and a handful of young women students into what is known today as Bethune-Cookman College. Her wisdom is what Franklin D. Roosevelt sought when he made her a part of his unofficial cabinet of advisors. It was wisdom that she dispensed when she wrote in her last will and testament:

> Sometimes I ask myself if I have any other legacy to leave. Truly, my worldly possessions are few. Yet my experiences have been rich. From them I have distilled principles and policies in which I believed firmly, for they represent the meaning of my life's work. They are the products of much sweat and sorrow. Perhaps, in them there is something of value. So as my life draws to a close, I will pass them on to Negroes everywhere in the hope that an old woman's philosophy may give them inspiration. Here then is my legacy. . . . I leave you love. . . . I leave you hope. . . . I leave you the challenge of developing confidence in one another. . . . I leave you a thirst for education. . . . I leave you respect for the use of power. . . . I leave you faith. . . . I leave you racial dignity. . . . I leave you a desire to live harmoniously with your fellow man. . . . I leave you finally, a responsibility to our young people.[5]

Mary McLeod Bethune was indeed a woman who was a major contributor to the cult of black womanhood. Born in 1875, Bethune founded the institution now known as Bethune-Cookman College, the only historically black college founded by an African American woman that continues to survive today. She was also a founder of the National Council of Negro Women, a thriving organization devoted to the improvement of conditions for women and children.

In 1904 in Florida, Bethune started the Daytona Educational and Industrial Institute, the predecessor to the college, "with five girls and a dollar and a half and faith in God." By 1920, forty-seven girls had completed the full high school course, and ten taught in the public school system in Florida. She later became an advisor to President Franklin D. Roosevelt's "Kitchen Cabinet." In her later years, Bethune traveled to Europe to champion the cause of African American women.[6]

There is no doubt that the life and work of Mary McLeod Bethune were undergirded by her deep sense of commitment to the cause of improving the plight of African Americans and that she sought wisdom from God to do it. As an example of what it meant to be a proponent of the ethic of black womanhood, Bethune stands out in front. She not only worked to re-create the ethos of African American women; she lived her life in an exemplary way, and she left trying to pass on what she had learned during that lifetime of service. It could readily be said about Mary McLeod Bethune, as it was said about the Queen of Sheba, that she was "inquisitive about life and serious-minded."[7]

The Story of the Queen of Sheba: A Queen's Search for Faith and Wisdom

Scripture Readings

The following are biblical references to the Queen of Sheba. Read them before beginning this chapter.

- The Queen of Sheba visits King Solomon to find out about the wisdom bestowed upon him by his God, Yahweh (1 Kings 10:1–10, 13; 2 Chron. 9:1–9, 12).
- Jesus tells the Pharisees that the Queen of the South will judge them at the end time (Matt. 12:42; Luke 11:31).

Introduction

According to Dr. Cain Hope Felder, it was around 620 B.C.E. that the deuteronomic editors introduced into the tenth chapter of First Kings the story of an obscure queen's visit to King Solomon, and three centuries later, the writers of Second Chronicles repeated it. Giving her the title of the Queen of Sheba, the writers used this foreign woman's story to provide an outsider's affirmation that God had fulfilled the promise to provide Solomon with wisdom and wealth if he was obedient (1 Kings 3:10–14). The writers were able to use the words of the Queen of Sheba to celebrate Solomon's wisdom, praise his God, and provide proof for all who inquired that the God of Israel was faithful.[1]

Yet in the midst of affirming Solomon's riches and wisdom, the mysterious and powerful queen became the subject of legends, religious traditions, and commentary. Throughout the centuries until the present day, some remnant of the Queen of Sheba's story has entered into the cultural and religious lives of the people of Ethiopia, Arabia, Europe, and Israel, as well as into the cultural ethos of African Americans. Whether one reads about the Queen of Sheba in Jewish midrash (commentary), Islamic literature, Ethiopian national and political history, Christian medieval writings, current-day Rastafarian popular culture, or African American sermons, the Queen of Sheba has crossed cultural and religious lines as a figure of intrigue and historical significance. Bursting with potential for speculation and interpretation, this fascinating African queen has been labeled as both historical and mythical; saint and sinner; beautiful and ugly; wise and foolish. However, Jesus set the record straight and gave her a role in God's plan of salvation. Consequently, the answer to the question, "Who is the Queen of Sheba?" depends upon who is being asked.

When we look at the various claims on her, it is no wonder that each has not only given her a different name but also assigned to her visit to King Solomon a different function and purpose. The Hebrew writers called her the Queen of Sheba; the Ethiopians called her Queen Makeda; the Muslims called her Belquis; and Josephus, the first-century historian, called her the Queen of Egypt and Ethiopia. However, Jesus called her the Queen of the South and assigned to her a role in God's salvific plan—a recognition that the queen's visit tested Solomon's wisdom and her inquisitiveness led others to acknowledge her wisdom.

The queen's origin, her journey to King Solomon, the hard questions she asked, her search for wisdom, and her praise of Solomon's God all contribute to the mystique that surrounds this African woman, who some believe personifies wisdom. What is so extraordinary about this story, about this woman, and about this visit that keeps the fascination alive centuries later? Even to this day, the narrative about the Queen of Sheba has found a place in the biblical studies of African American women. For despite the debates surrounding her nationality, her character, and her historical or mythical status, black women have claimed her as their own. For them, she is an African queen who embarked upon a long journey to King Solomon—seeking God, understanding, and truth. Such a faith journey speaks to their lives in intimate and profound ways.

Moreover, in a Bible that is full of women as prostitutes, adulteresses, harlots, concubines, and every once in a while judges or prophets, the queen stands out as the ideal woman. She is a woman of courage, independence, and perseverance who travels a long distance seeking wisdom and religious understanding. In this respect she is the biblical mentor to Sojourner Truth, Mary McLeod Bethune, Ida B. Wells Barnett, and many other black women who embarked upon peculiar journeys into unfamiliar territory searching for truth. With her own kingdom, her own wealth, and her visit to Solomon on her own terms, she can be characterized using the words of the first African American woman in the U.S. Congress, Shirley Chisholm, as being "unbossed and unbought."[2]

Other black women have used her as an example of a wise and virtuous woman whom they seek to emulate. "How we delight to repeat the story of the Queen of Sheba and that long and tedious journey she took seeking after truth," preached Florence Spearing Randolph in the early years of the twentieth century. Randolph was "among a small group of [African American] women evangelists licensed to preach and ordained as deacons and elders in the late nineteenth century" by the African Methodist Episcopal Zion Church.[3]

Of course, Randolph was only echoing what would become other black women's fascination with the biblical story about a long journey, a search for faith, and a persistent inquisitiveness that sought to gain the truth. For African American women who sought to re-create and redefine their womanhood, wisdom became a virtue that they sought through education and religious understanding. Many saw themselves as the writers of the *Kebra Nagast*[4] saw the queen when they quoted her as saying before leaving for Israel:

> For I desire wisdom and my heart seeketh to find understanding. I am smitten with the love of wisdom, for wisdom is far better than treasures of gold and silver, and wisdom is the best of everything that hath been created on the earth. Unto what under the heavens shall wisdom be compared? It is sweeter than honey and it makes one to rejoice more than wine; it shines more than the sun and it is beloved more than precious stones. It fattens more than oil, and it satisfies more than dainty meats, and it gives more fame than thousands of gold and silver. It is a source of joy for the heart, a bright and shining light for the eyes and a giver of speed to the feet; a shield for the breast and a helmet for the head.[5]

Just like the life of the Queen of Sheba, or Queen Makeda, the lives of black women have been lived in search of faith and understanding—lives characterized by long journeys and hard questions. Even as African American women embarked upon such journeys, they encountered resistance and criticism as well as a world that misunderstood their motives and was suspicious of their ambition. That was what happened to the Queen of Sheba. Evidence of these misconceptions, misunderstandings, and misinterpretations of the queen's life and journey can be found in traditional commentaries on the story.

The remainder of this chapter will retell the story of the Queen of Sheba, briefly review some of the traditional commentaries, and using a justice reading strategy, look at the story as a part of a broader worldview. Chapter 12 offers reflection questions on her and her story.

The Story

The Scripture tells us that the Queen of Sheba did the following: she came to test the king with difficult questions (riddles); she brought gifts of gold and precious stones; she told him what was on her mind; she observed all of Solomon's wisdom and the riches of his house; she acknowledged her doubt and confessed her new belief, while praising God. Solomon, in turn, gave the queen her every desire before she returned home.

The Queen of Sheba's account of Solomon's blessings is mentioned in detail and is generally the account most used to verify his wealth and wisdom. Another unique aspect of the story is that for a king whose downfall is foreign women and their gods, Solomon's interaction with the Queen of Sheba is just the opposite. She comes not to be one of his wives or concubines, but as a leader of a people. She engages him in questions as the other male leaders and kings have done and then praises his God. She goes away, praising the God of Israel, an act that places her on the opposite spectrum of the other one thousand foreign women in Solomon's life. Whereas the other foreign women are dependent upon him, and for them, he indulges their gods to his own detriment, the Queen of Sheba is independent of him with her own sovereignty and appears to abandon her god and praises his.

Scripturally, the queen's visit is placed before the announcement about the fate of Solomon (1 Kings 11:1–13) and before his death (1 Kings 11:41–42) and the subsequent demise of his kingdom (1 Kings 12). It is the last affirming statement about his wealth coming from an outsider. While the narrative that follows the queen's visit describes the gifts of Solomon, the queen's account has endured as the final witness to his riches and wisdom—God's promised blessings to him.

The Queen of Sheba reappears in the Gospels as Jesus rebukes the Pharisees for asking for a sign of the times proclaiming him as the Messiah. Having performed many miracles and healings, Jesus cautions the Pharisees that the Queen of the South will condemn them in the end time because she had the character and courage to travel to the ends of the earth to test Solomon. Her actions compared to those of the doubting Pharisees earned her a place in God's plan of salvation.

This is the extent of the biblical story about the Queen of Sheba's visit to King Solomon. It is not, however, the end of the story because surrounding this unique but simple Hebrew story are other stories from cultures for whom the Queen of Sheba's visit played a significant role in their cultural, political, and religious history. These other stories include the rendition of the Ethiopian national narrative found in the *Kebra Nagast,* the Jewish rabbinical writings included in the Jewish Midrash, the medieval fables and tales known as *Pseudo Ben Sira,* and the Islamic sacred book, the Qur'an. Many traditional commentaries on the story arise from a combination of excerpts from one or more of these sources.

The Queen of Sheba in Salvation History

Rich with part history, part myth, the stories surrounding the Queen of Sheba far surpass the time devoted to her visit to King Solomon in the Hebrew Scriptures, contributing much to the fascination over the years with this woman who sought understanding and wisdom. Symbolically, the Queen of Sheba represents Mother Wisdom for feminist theologians. The queen serves as the embodiment of the wisdom references in the Song of Solomon and in the Proverbs. With all of the stories surrounding the queen's visit, her purpose, and her relationship with Solomon, it is easy to understand why many readers of the Gospels are surprised to hear Jesus speak of her while chastising the Pharisees. Jesus' remarks are significant in clearing up the biblical role of the queen. Jesus affirms her place in the history of a people, and he gives her a place in God's salvific plan. What is it about the queen's journey that Jesus acknowledges?

Her search and her persistent attempts to discover what the Hebrew God had done for the people of Israel through their king made Jesus take note of her journey. Her discernment and wisdom made her stand out as an exemplar of the faithful. Jesus applauds and rewards her search for truth and faith by making her one who will judge the faithless, who are not seekers.

In the final analysis, the queen's character brings her into the Gospels. When Jesus tells the Pharisees that she will be the one to judge their generation in the end time, he is speaking more of the character traits that she exhibited. She came a long distance, says Jesus, to seek out the wisdom of King Solomon, and here are these characterless people, the Pharisees, with someone greater than Solomon in their midst and yet they ask for a sign.

Usually a champion of the disinherited and the oppressed, Jesus has claimed, as a part of God's salvific plan, an African queen as one who will judge at the end time: "The queen of the South will rise at the judgment with the people of this generation and condemn them, because she came from the ends of the earth to listen to the wisdom of Solomon, and see, something greater than Solomon is here!" (Luke 11:31). So no matter what the scholars have said about her, or the writers of antiquity say about her, like African American women, Jesus defines who she is. Black women have had to depend upon this image of a woman strong enough to seek the truth and faithful enough to be called by Jesus as a judge at the end time. Such an assurance—that the world cannot define who they are or what their peculiar faith journey means—has kept black women faithful. But Jesus can define them as having a special place within God's salvific plan, and they can become whole. Mary McLeod Bethune taught these lessons to the girls who went through her school. A redirection of their lives would be the consequence of a redefinition of who they were as women seeking wisdom, truth, and faith.

Traditional Commentary

Then she said, "You are a wise man. Would you be able to answer the question of mine were I to put it to you?" He responded: "For the Lord gives wisdom; from His mouth comes knowledge and understanding." And so, she asked: "What are they? Seven depart and nine enter, two give drink, but only one partakes." He responded, "No doubt, seven are the days of the menstrual cycle, nine are the months of pregnancy, two [refers] to the breasts that succor and one to the child born [who drinks from them]."

"You are a wise man! Would you be able to answer another question of mine were I to put it to you?" He responded (as before), "For the Lord gives wisdom." And so, she asked: "What does it signify? A woman says to her son, 'Your father is my father. Your grandfather is my husband. You are my son and I am your sister.'" He answered her, "No doubt, the daughters of Lot."[6]

This excerpt from the Jewish Midrash to the book of Proverbs is typical of the type of sexually oriented questions it was speculated that the queen asked the king. For writers of the wisdom literature, riddles were used to test true wisdom. Riddles such as these were inserted in the Jewish Midrash to Proverbs as a way of substantiating Solomon's blessings of discernment and wisdom. However, this is also a good example of the kind of comments that have followed the story of the Queen of Sheba. Many of these comments center on sexual questions as well as questions challenging her femininity.

Contemporary writers regard these disparaging comments as a way of belittling the strong figure of a woman monarch. Because she is a woman of independence, intellect, and power, the traditionalists have tended to downplay the spiritual, economic, or intellectual nature of her trip. Rather, they have heightened their speculation to embody a sexual encounter or to assign masculine qualities to the queen. For example, in some of the writings, the queen is pictured as a woman who had hairy legs like a man; in others, she is pictured as a deformed woman or considered an evil woman with deformed feet.

In the medieval writings known as *Pseudo Ben Sira,* the following exchange takes place between Nebuchadnezzar and the sage Ben Sira:

> When your mother, the queen of Sheba arrived with tribute to listen to Solomon's wisdom, he found her beautiful and wished to have intercourse with her. But he found her exceedingly hairy—that was a time when no Israelite woman had hair on those parts of her body ordinarily covered by garments. And so, Solomon declared to his servants, "Bring me lime and arsenic." They took the lime (solution) and sifted it in a sieve. Then they ground the arsenic and mixed the two together. They did this so that when Solomon then saw your mother, her skin was made

pure and completely free of hair. Following that, he did with her as he wished.[7]

It is clear from these commentaries that the Queen of Sheba had stepped across some gender lines that made it difficult for Jewish scholars and medieval writers to accept the fact that she visited Solomon to further her religious, political, and perhaps economic interests, separate from her sexual desires. The sexism that created these negative comments about the queen is well documented in a book by Jacob Lassner, *Demonizing the Queen of Sheba*. Lassner's research shows that a conscious effort was made to portray the queen negatively. This could have been to prevent other women from feeling empowered to take bold actions in the midst of men. In speaking about his book Lassner states:

> To be more precise, it asks how and why the historic event, a diplomatic mission recorded by the biblical chronicler, was reshaped by later Jewish and Muslim writers to accommodate contemporary values and newly defined concerns. By the Middle Ages, the main focus of the queen's visit had shifted from international to sexual politics and from diplomatic relations to the more complicated relations between men and women. That is, in its post biblical and Islamic versions, the queen's joust with Solomon was portrayed as a dangerous attempt to subvert time-honored rules of gender.[8]

Perhaps one of the most significant attempts to recast the Queen of Sheba has come from those who would try to question her nationality out of a need to de-emphasize or deconstruct her African designation. The historian Josephus describes the Queen of Sheba as "Queen of Egypt and Ethiopia; she was inquisitive into philosophy and one that on other accounts also was to be admired."[9]

In his book *Blacks in Antiquity*, Dr. Frank Snowden Jr. provides some historical support for the collaboration between Egypt and Ethiopia over the course of the Solomonic reign and into the eighth century B.C.E. According to his research, Ethiopia was a major military force in Africa, having colonized Egypt for more than half a century.[10] While

Snowden makes this important connection between Ethiopia and Egypt, other writers keep the two separate. Many of their comments find their way into the writings that speak of the Queen of Sheba's having been a queen of Arabia (modern-day Yemen).[11] Ironically, each of these research results regarding this mysterious queen has deep roots in the stories of both Ethiopian culture and Arab culture. Both have claimed her as their own. Known to the Ethiopians as Queen Makeda and to the Arabs as Belquis, this woman of means and power occupies a significant role in the religious and cultural history of both peoples. Unfortunately, many of the commentaries on the queen are not without their own cultural biases.

A review of these commentaries makes it evident that not only is the queen denied the dignity and respect of a visiting head of state—one with a legacy that far outdated that of Solomon—but Western-dominated scholarship has also denied her nationality. Describing the Queen of Sheba as an Arab, rather than an Ethiopian, diluted her African identity and denied some of the strong cultural, religious, and national history of the Ethiopian people. For some theologians it was a better cultural comfort zone than what the black-skinned Ethiopian peoples could have provided.

This is not to say that the Arabs did not stake their claim to the queen. Naming her Belquis, the Qur'an speaks of the queen's visit as symbolic of the soul in search of Allah. The queen and king are disembodied mystical figures searching for spiritual fulfillment. Once the queen finds fulfillment by the spirit, she submits to Solomon. The story is one of submission to the will of Allah.

Ironically, it is in the commentaries of John Calvin that the queen is restored to her Ethiopian heritage. Calvin writes:

> As Ethiopia lies in the southerly direction from Judea, I willingly concur with Josephus and other writers, who assert that she was the queen of Ethiopia. In sacred history she is called, the queen of Sheba. We must not suppose this Sheba to be the country of Saba, which rather lay toward the east, but a town situated in Meroe, an island on the Nile, which was the metropolis of the kingdom.[12]

Other texts, such as the *Harper's Bible Dictionary,* disagree with Calvin. These sources speak of the queen coming from Seba (Saba), a trading post in southeast Arabia that was colonized by Ethiopia. Most traditional Western documents tend to support the *Harper's* finding; however, new and more diverse scholarship continues to point to a woman of African descent.[13]

Finally, the African church father Origen spoke of the theological significance of the Queen of Sheba's visit as part of a thread of symbolism that centers on Ethiopia as the end of the earth. He uses as examples the Ethiopian eunuch, Moses' Midianite wife, and the biblical passages stating that Ethiopia will stretch out its arms to God. These, Origen believes, were all redemptive references meaning that Ethiopia had joined the ranks of the believers of God and had thus become eligible for salvation.[14]

Origen sees in the Queen of Sheba's visit to Solomon a parallel to the person of the church. He equates her visit to Solomon with the person of the church that comes to Christ from out of the Gentiles.

> In fulfillment of the type represented by the queen of Sheba, an Ethiopian, the Church comes from the Gentiles to hear the wisdom of the true Solomon and the true lover of Peace. She came to Jerusalem with a great following, not with a single nation as the Synagogue before her with Hebrews only, but she was accompanied by the races of the whole world offering worthy gifts to Christ. When this black and beautiful Queen had seen all in the House of the King of Peace, she expressed her amazement. But Origen concludes, when she comes to the heavenly Jerusalem she will see wonders more numerous and splendid.[15]

All of these commentaries on the queen that stem from the very simple story in the Hebrew Scriptures and the Gospel reference of Jesus can be summarized by the words of Paul House in his 1995 commentary:

> Various interpretations of this story arose over time, Jewish, Ethiopic, and Christian circles. One Jewish legend holds that Solomon fathered a son for the queen, which was her ultimate

"desire." Ethiopic tradition parallels the Jewish tradition, for it claims "the royal Abyssinian line was founded by the offspring of Solomon and the queen of Sheba." Neither of these traditions has any historical basis, nor can they be substantiated by the biblical text. Jesus uses the queen as an example of the effort one should be willing to make to hear God's truth (Matthew 12:42). She traveled 1,500 miles to question Solomon, but Jesus's audience refuses to listen to the Son of God himself.[16]

With all of this commentary and these analyses, the Queen of Sheba remains a mystery. Although this next section cannot answer all of the questions regarding the queen, it does provide another perspective for a more holistic approach to portraying this enigmatic African woman.

Justice Reading Strategy: The Ethiopian Kebra Nagast and Queen Makeda

Probably the most enduring image of the Queen of Sheba outside the Hebrew Scriptures is that provided by the Ethiopians in their national sacred book, the Kebra Nagast. Giving her the name Queen Makeda, the Kebra Nagast (the Glory of the Kings) is essentially the story of the queen and King Solomon and the son that they are said to have parented, Menelik I.

The Kebra Nagast begins in Ethiopia where the queen is said to have received reports from one of her merchants of the wealth and wisdom of the new king Solomon. The merchant, Tamrin, reports to Queen Makeda (the Queen of Sheba) that Solomon is "the richest King on earth, who ruled with the wisdom of a sage. Tamrin repeats the story almost daily, giving examples of how Solomon rules his vast kingdom with a wise system."[17]

Upon hearing this report, the queen embarks upon her journey. It is perhaps Tamrin's account that provides the basis for the opening line of the scriptures: "When the queen of Sheba heard of the fame of Solomon (fame due to the name of God), she came to test him with hard questions" (1 Kings 10:1). She takes the long, arduous trip because the queen herself is a seeker of wisdom.

She is reported to have said,

And without wisdom that which the tongue speaks is not acceptable. Wisdom is the best of all treasures. He who heaps up gold and silver does so to no profit without wisdom, but he who heaps up wisdom no man can snatch it from his heart. That which fools heap up, the wise consume. And because of the wickedness of those who do evil, the righteous are praised; and because of the wicked acts of fools the wise are beloved. So I will follow the footprints of wisdom and it shall protect me forever.[18]

On her way to Israel, the queen stops in Sheba, one of her provinces. It is perhaps from this stop that she gains the label "the Queen of Sheba." After much festivity she leaves Sheba and journeys to Jerusalem. The queen's visit, once she is in the presence of Solomon, is the subject of much discussion, more so in the Kebra Nagast than in the Bible. The Ethiopian text states that the queen spent six months at Solomon's palace after traveling for fifteen hundred miles.

In the Ethiopian version, then, there are two reasons for the queen's journey. First, she hears about the fame of Solomon. His abilities earn him the reputation of being the wisest man in the ancient world (1 Kings 4:29–34). This very rich, very successful, and curious woman intends to see if he deserves such acclaim. Second, she comes because of Solomon's God. In other words, she recognizes that only a great God could produce such a great king.

Yet she seeks spiritual insight from one famous for possessing the wisdom coming from God. The stage is set for a meeting of a queen and a king who will generate centuries of speculation and imaginative narratives, inspire art and national and religious identity. The words in the Hebrew Scriptures gain new insightful meaning when placed side by side with the writings of the Kebra Nagast. For example, the queen is said to have "marveled in her heart and was utterly astonished in her mind, and she recognized in her understanding and perceived very clearly with her eyes how admirable he was."[19]

The king was also taken by the queen's curiosity, and according to the story, he spent days trying to convert her to Judaism. He succeeded in doing that, and she made plans to return home. It is here, after the conversion, that the Kebra Nagast begins the love story.

Solomon is said to have tricked the queen into sleeping on one side of the tent, making her promise that she would not take anything of value from him. That night before going to bed he feeds her a very spicy dish and tells one of his servants to place a jar of water near her bed. She awakes in the middle of the night and looks at the king to see if he is asleep. He feigns sleep, and she takes a drink of the water. The king accuses her of taking valuable water from him, and the consequences of her actions result in his taking her to bed with him.

Out of this union is born Menelik I, who later goes on to rule Ethiopia and to receive from Solomon the ark of the covenant. This dynasty that originates with Menelik is culminated in the reign of Haile Selassie I (1892–1975). Haile Selassie I, whose name means "Power of the Holy Trinity," was born Ras Tafari Makonnen and reigned as the emperor of Ethiopia from 1930 to 1936. After Ethiopia was invaded by Italy in 1935, he initially fought but then fled and went into exile until his triumphant return in 1941. He remained emperor, albeit through minor coups, until 1974, when he was overthrown and placed in prison. He died in 1975. He is celebrated by the current-day Rastafarian movement. This religious and cultural movement honors the rule of Haile Selassie I as the last of the Solomonic kings. He inherited the titles "King of Kings, Lord of Lords, Elect of God, Conquering Lion of the tribe of Judah. . . . He was the 225th rebirth of Solomon and direct descendant of the union of King Solomon and the Queen of Sheba."[20]

Some scholars believe that the proof of the queen's religious reforms can also be traced through the 1984 airlift of Ethiopian Jews rescued from famine in their homeland by Israeli pilots. These Ethiopian Jews, known as Falashas, have a long and intriguing history. They practice Jewish rituals, read from the Pentateuch, and claim to have the ark of the covenant within their homeland. Folklore has it that their ancestors accompanied Menelik I to Jerusalem to recover the ark, and upon returning home, a segment of those who accompanied Menelik separated and became more orthodox. There is, however, no conclusive information regarding the origin of the Falashas. Like the Queen of Sheba, they remain a mystery.[21]

Thus, the queen's legacy lives on in the national literature and cultural and religious context of Ethiopia. She has been embraced by the culture as the matriarch of the Solomonic dynasty and the founding spiritual leader for their monotheistic faith tradition.

Conclusion

> I went in through the door of the treasury of wisdom and I drew for myself the waters of understanding. . . . Through wisdom I have dived down into the great sea and have seized in the place of wisdom's depth, a great pearl whereby I am rich. I went down like the great iron anchor whereby men anchor ships for the night on the high seas, and I received a lamp which lighteth me, and I came up by the ropes of the boat of understanding. I went to sleep in the depths of the sea, and not being overwhelmed with the water I dreamed a dream. And it seemed to me that there was a star in my womb and I marveled there at and I laid hold upon it, and it lighted me with splendor thereof.[22]

The queen's description of her trip is perhaps the most intriguing and the most poetic. It not only sparks the imagination, but it also maintains the wisdom quest and hints at her version of what may have resulted in the birth of Menelik I. Whatever happened on the trip, the queen returned to Ethiopia and instituted the Jewish religious tradition. She is said to have gone back to Ethiopia and established religious reforms renouncing the gods of Ethiopia and mandating the worship of God.

> Love ye what is right and hate falsehood, for what is right is righteousness and falsehood is the head of iniquity. And ye shall not use fraud and oppression among yourselves for God dwelleth with you and the habitation of his Glory is among you. For you have become members of His household. And from this time onward cease ye to observe your former customs, namely making auguries from birds, and from signs and from magic.

And if after this day there be found any man who observeth all his former customs, his house shall be plundered and ye and his wife and his children shall be condemned.[23]

In the end, the Queen of Sheba's story has accompanied the Solomon narrative throughout the world. She was a woman of courage and was admired for her wisdom.

Reflecting on the
Queen of Sheba

This chapter includes questions for reflection on the story of the Queen of Sheba as well as scriptural references for biblical reflections on the virtue of wisdom. These questions can be used as a part of a group Bible study, or they can be used as part of a personal spiritual growth and development discipline.

Reflection Questions on the Queen of Sheba and Wisdom

The following biblical references to wisdom can be used for further biblical reflection on wisdom as a virtue, wisdom as a characteristic of God, and wisdom as female. These scriptures can also be used as personal ethical guidance and as a key to the Bible's wisdom literature.

    1. Wisdom as a virtue:

> Job 33:33
> Proverbs 2
> Proverbs 13:10, 20

1 Corinthians 12:8
Ephesians 1:17

2. Wisdom as a characteristic of God:

Job 9:4
Daniel 2:20–23
Romans 11:33
1 Corinthians 1:18–31
Ephesians 3:10

3. Wisdom as female imagery:

Proverbs 8
Proverbs 9:1–6
Wisdom of Solomon 6:12–25
Wisdom of Solomon 7:1–14
Sirach 15:1–10

4. The Queen of Sheba's reputation has suffered primarily because there are those who felt that a woman in such a powerful role had no place in God's salvation plan. Can you relate to having been criticized and maligned just because you were "inquisitive and serious-minded"? How did you respond? How would you recast your response in light of the Christian witness exhibited in this section of the book?

5. Are there women in your life you would describe as women of wisdom? Find one and listen to her story about her faith journey. What can you learn from her? How does it compare with your journey?

part five

PERSEVERANCE

Therefore, since we are surrounded by so great a cloud of witnesses, let us also lay aside every weight and the sin that clings so closely, and let us run with perseverance the race that is set before us, looking to Jesus the pioneer and perfecter of our faith, who for the sake of the joy that was set before him endured the cross, disregarding its shame, and has taken his seat at the right hand of the throne of God. (Heb. 12:1–2)

Perseverance as a Virtue and Fannie Lou Hamer

Perseverance has been defined as remaining steadfast in our faith against all odds. The Scripture provides not only instructions for perseverance of the faithful, but in the life of Jesus and later martyrdom of his followers, we are given examples of what it means to be steadfast in the faith. Whether it was John who refused to compromise the truth to save his life or the witness and testimony of Paul or Peter or the countless thousands of martyrs who died because of their faith, perseverance stands out as a Christian virtue that reaps the reward of eternal life.

This reward of eternal life for those who endure to the end is available to all believers. However, some doctrines hold that this is available only to a select few. For example, Calvinists hold fast to the doctrine of John Calvin, who considers perseverance to be the steadfast faith of the "elect" who withstand the tribulations of life and receive salvation based on predestination. Calvin's use of the term "elect" refers to a particular theology of predestination, which is the belief that before time God selected or elected certain people who would receive salvation, regardless of how they lived their lives. Many theologians refute this interpretation and believe that the election was actually God's election of Jesus, who became flesh on earth in order to atone for the sins of all humanity. This eliminates the belief that just an arbitrary select few were chosen by God. While God did the choosing of the Hebrew people, the choice carried with it the responsibility for the chosen to make known to the world the work of a just God.

Thus, those who persevere, who hold fast to the end, include all believers. They are the "cloud of witnesses," who have run the race of the faithful and endured the tragedies of life while still remaining true to God, who affirm this belief. That God sacrificed once and for all is sufficient to give every believer this chance at salvation.

When we look at the African American faith journey, endurance and perseverance are irrefutable virtues that have found a place in the struggle toward freedom. There are no shortages of exemplars of this virtue. However, one woman's journey highlights the public display of a persevering spirit. If any African American woman exhibited perseverance, it was Fannie Lou Hamer, the sharecropper who founded a political party. Her enduring battle to gain voting rights for Mississippi blacks during the 1960s is legendary. One of the founders of the Mississippi Freedom Democratic Party (MFDP), Fannie Lou Hamer combined her religious fervor with the struggle for human rights and in the process made life better for those who would follow her. Noted not only for her political activism, but also for her strong spiritual presence, Fannie Lou Hamer would generally sing "This Little Light of Mine" before she began her speeches. It was a trademark of her presentations, and it spoke to her boundless faith in God's ability to use a sharecropper to change a nation.

Born Fannie Lou Townsend in 1917 in Montgomery County, Mississippi, she was the youngest of twenty children. At the age of six she began sharecropping, picking cotton, and working the farm like her parents before her. From 1923 to 1962, Fannie Lou Hamer's life appeared to be destined to end in the fields of Mississippi, eking out a living as a sharecropper, a second-class citizen, without any rights and privileges of a U.S. citizen, namely, the right to vote. That would have been her fate except that something happened in 1962. The civil rights movement had taken hold, and Fannie Lou Hamer, caught up in the southern momentum of the movement, wanted to exercise the South's elusive "right to vote." It changed her reality and expanded her horizons, leading to a life that would be devoted to change and justice in the midst of danger, imprisonment, and violence. Fannie Lou Hamer persevered with a visible faith and a determination that made her a legend in the struggle to enfranchise African Americans.

Tireless in her efforts to fight the then prevailing system of disenfranchisement, Hamer endured beatings, personal terrorism, economic reprisals, and death threats. Those tactics, however, were no match for her thirst for freedom and her determination to get it. Her most famous quote, "I'm sick and tired of being sick and tired," should in no way indicate that Fannie Lou Hamer was ready at any point along the way to quit. Quite the contrary, she was a voice to be reckoned with up until her death in 1977. From being a sharecropper to founder of a political party, Fannie Lou Hamer lived a life described by the term "liberation theology." She believed and promoted the belief that God was on the side of the oppressed and that God would deliver and transform the hearts of the southern politicians, so that human rights would be the norm, not the exception.

In *Black Women in America,* an encyclopedia on African American women, a 1965 interview quotes Fannie Lou Hamer as saying:

I do remember, one time a man came to me after the students began to work in Mississippi, and he said the white people were getting tired and they were getting tense and anything might happen. Well, I asked him, "How long he thinks we had been getting tired?" I have been tired for forty six years, my parents was tired before me, and their parents were tired; and I have always wanted to do something that would help some of the things I would see going on among Negroes that I didn't like and I don't like now.[1]

In looking at the Gospel story about the Canaanite woman and the courage and perseverance that she exhibited in the scripture, we may see the spirit in her that is also present in Fannie Lou Hamer. Petitioning Jesus to heal her sick child, the Canaanite woman seemed to say to Jesus, "I will not go away until you perform a blessing for me because I am sick and tired of being sick and tired."

The Story of the Canaanite Woman: A Persevering Spirit Encounters Jesus

Scripture Readings

The following are biblical references to the Canaanite woman. Read them before beginning this chapter.

- Two passages tell the story of the Canaanite woman (Syrophoenician in Mark) who begs Jesus to cure her demon-possessed daughter (Matt. 15:21–28; Mark 7:24–30). Jesus calls her people dogs and initially declines to heal her daughter, but the woman perseveres.

Introduction

This scripture about Jesus and the Canaanite woman (Syrophoenician woman in Mark) has always posed a dilemma for readers because of the nature of Jesus' response. It is an uncharacteristic Jesus who responds so harshly to the Canaanite woman. Where is the compassionate Jesus? Where is the healing Jesus? Where is the Jesus who embraces all outcasts? Where is the divine side of Jesus? All of these are valid questions that can and should be raised about Jesus' encounter with the Canaanite woman. This chapter will look at the woman and the character traits that she possesses as well as at Jesus' initial and final responses to her. Unfolding throughout this story is the unraveling of the mission of Jesus, a mission that will change the course of history with this woman's contribution evident in that transformation.

How important is the woman's persevering spirit? How significant is her ethnicity? How unique is her encounter with Jesus? Many traditional commentators avoid these questions and focus on the faith of the woman, but it is clear that there is more to this story than the faith of the woman. On the hope that she holds out for her daughter's suffering and Jesus' response hangs the question of how inclusive the salvation story will become.

The remainder of the chapter will retell the story of the Canaanite woman, using the Matthew text, review her role in salvation history, present an overview of traditional commentaries, and using a justice reading strategy, look at how this woman's story can open new vistas for understanding the gospel message. Chapter 15 offers reflection questions on the story.

The Story

After traveling, Jesus is ready to rest, and out of seemingly nowhere appears this Canaanite woman who lived in the area. The woman cries out to Jesus and calls him the "Son of David," telling him that her daughter is tormented by a demon. Jesus initially does not answer her at all. He ignores her cry for help and healing.

The disciples, in an effort to follow in Jesus' footsteps and get rid of the woman, tell him to send her away because she keeps shouting after them. In an unusual response, Jesus tells her that he was sent to help only the Israelites, "the lost sheep of the house of Israel."

Undeterred, the woman asks Jesus again to help her. This third answer is the one that causes much consternation among Christians. Jesus tells her that her people are dogs, and it is not fair to take the children's food and "throw it to the dogs." Referring to his lost sheep of Israel, Jesus is declaring the Jewish people to be the children of God and her people (the Canaanites or Syrophoenicians) to be outside God's direct blessings, receiving instead what is left over (the crumbs). The woman perseveres and will not let Jesus dismiss her or her people in such a way: "Yes, Lord, yet even the dogs eat the crumbs that fall from their masters' table." This retort earns the woman a fourth response from Jesus. This one is more in character with the compassionate, healing Jesus. He tells her to go home; he performs the miracle from afar and heals her daughter.

Interpretations of this scripture usually focus on the faith of the woman, but as will be seen in the following sections, there is more to the story than her faithfulness.

Traditional Commentaries

As is evident from the text, Jesus has an uncharacteristically virulent response to this woman of color. He initially refuses to acknowledge her petition to heal her demon-possessed daughter. The woman is undaunted; she is determined, defiant, and rebellious. Jesus, she determines, will live up to his broader mission—a mission heretofore defined as a ministry to Jews alone. Jesus relents and, upon commenting on her faith, commands the woman to go home, her daughter is healed.

This woman is an equally important symbol in Mark's Gospel. There she is called a Syrophoenician woman rather than a Canaanite woman. The distinction is important because the message that each writer wants to send to the reader is satisfied by these two designations. Mark's more contemporary label paints a quick picture of a woman of mixed race, coming from a conquered people, a second-class citizen in a country that once belonged to her people. Matthew, it appears, is attempting to maintain continuity with the witness of the Hebrew Scriptures; although Mark appears to want to let the current political situation be acknowledged, he wants to move quickly toward the emerging new covenant in Jesus Christ.

Matthew labels the woman Canaanite, evoking the historical adversarial relationship of the people of Israel and the Hamitic people of Canaan. Some historians see them as the same people, separated because of the Egyptian enslavement and reunited as different people when Joshua enters Canaan. As a matter of fact, Hebrew, the language, is a dialect of the Canaanite language.[1]

Of course, it also makes the point more profoundly when Jesus turns from his stated mission to the Jews to include a healing event for this particular racial Gentile. Her ethnicity is important to the story because the Canaanite label targets her immediately as a pagan, an enemy of the Jews, or an unwanted outcast.

> The use of Canaanite rather than Syro-Phoenician as in Mark 7:26 emphasizes that the woman comes from an ethnicity traditionally an enemy of Israel worthy of extermination. The story of the Canaanite woman shows that Jesus himself can initially fail to perceive faith and thereby refuse access to the kingdom to those to whom he was sent. Jesus, an Israelite man, allows himself to be duped by the appearance of this supplicant as a woman and a non-Israelite.[2]

The response to the Canaanite woman is a challenge not only for the human Jesus, but also for his disciples who, out of nationalistic fervor, admonish Jesus to turn the woman away. It could be expected that Mark would employ the obtuse disciples in this manner, but the Matthean scripture is consistent with earlier explanations in chapter 10, where Jesus specifically calls upon the disciples to minister only to the Jews. The temptation to place Jewish nationalism at the core of the gospel is overcome by the presence of this woman of color. "These twelve Jesus sent out with the following instructions: 'Go nowhere among the Gentiles, and enter no town of the Samaritans, but go rather to the lost sheep of the house of Israel. As you go, proclaim the good news, "The realm of heaven has come near." Cure the sick, raise the dead, cleanse the lepers, cast out demons. You received without payment; give without payment'" (Matt. 10:5–8).

By the time he encounters the Canaanite woman (Matt. 15), Jesus has already established the parameters for the performance of miracles and the spread of the good news. Why is Jesus refusing this woman? The answer could very well rest in the unique claims of Jesus' fully divine, fully human nature. The fully human Jesus is a victim, as are other Jews, of a historic context that shapes his response to a former foe. Thus, given this context, it stands to reason that his response to the initial petitions of the woman would be a refusal to listen to her plea for expelling demons from her daughter. But Jesus' response even goes beyond the Matthean theme—which up to this point has been to give the gospel a universal appeal, while at the same time convincing his Jewish audience that Jesus is the promised Messiah of the Hebrew Scriptures.

How should these initial contradictions be compared to Jesus' final response to the Canaanite woman? Some scholars believe that Jesus meant that the prohibition against Gentiles was temporary, thus allowing for the introduction of the story of the Canaanite woman as the literary vehicle for the transformation of the gospel message to an audience beyond the Jews. With this interpretation, it is easy to see how Jesus could have used the Canaanite woman as a way of changing the temporary command and making a switch to include Gentiles as well as Jews. What follows is the possibility that the woman's daughter is healed by her faith, and the words of Jesus can appear to be just a way of exacting that confession of faith from her.

Matthew mentions the woman's faith. The faith of a woman in this Jew of prophecy casts another light on the story and provides another lesson for the disciples who are present in the Matthean account. Jesus has just shown the disciples that this Gentile has faith without being a preferred follower of Christ. Jesus has a mission that is expanding and unfolding in front of the disciples. This is a revelation that is brought about by an outsider.

As the disciples look on, Jesus changes his mission as he responds to this woman of color and saves her child. The woman is considered "by culture and language a Greek, by religion a pagan, by position in her community a nobody."[3]

More gender- and ethnic-conscious commentaries paint a more liberating picture of this woman. Her actions are not just those of the faithful, as has been traditionally acknowledged. The poignancy of her petition gives it relevance in the manifestation of the gospel today. One such commentator responds as follows:

> The woman responds out of a different cultural context. For her it is not a matter of sequence but of simultaneity. "In our culture," she explains, "the children and the house dogs eat at the same time." By changing the cultural context, the woman appeals to the experience of her people; they were receiving the benefits of Jesus' ministry before he even left Galilee. They went to him before he came to them. There is enough healing for everyone all at the same time. No one need be deprived or made to wait. . . . The woman completes her rhetorical coup and wins the argument. The woman's effective sermon achieves its goal; the unclean spirit leaves her daughter. Having made clean all foods in the previous section, the Markan Jesus now makes clean all races and peoples. It is worth noting that according to Mark, this anonymous woman won a place at the table not merely for her daughter, but for every Gentile Christian who reads these words.[4]

The perseverance of the Canaanite woman, a woman of African descent, has been one of the stories handed down throughout the black community as a story about faith. So great is the faith of the Canaanite woman that even though Jesus rebukes her and calls her people dogs, she continues to believe in his power to heal her daughter. The perseverance that she exhibits even at the height of her humiliation by Jesus speaks to the lengths to which a mother will go for her child. This perseverance, in spite of degrading circumstances, addresses the core of the virtues that black women have had to internalize in order to survive in a country that humiliated them and considered their people dogs. But despite this they stood fast for their children and brought about miracles for children whose only hope was death. Their pleas to God and their encounters on their knees have served as a testimony and a witness to their faith.

There are many "clouds of witnesses" to the fact that, like the faith of the Canaanite woman, their great faith has made their children whole.

The Canaanite Woman's Role in God's Salvation Plan

Perseverance at times is the only refuge for the disinherited, so the Canaanite woman perseveres in a story that is pivotal in the biblical message. It marks a decidedly important turning point in Jesus' earthly ministry. Jesus departs from a plan that called upon his disciples to minister only to Jews and embarks upon a more inclusive ministry that spreads to the Gentiles as well. Once again an outsider, an African woman of faith, changes the proscription for salvation and places in the salvation story the possibility that others will share in God's goodness. Another Canaanite woman, Rahab, who became the first convert in the promised land, made a similar impact on the future of the Hebrews.

Many people look at the Canaanite woman's treatment by Jesus and begin to pity the plight of this woman for whom the healing of her daughter meant her own humiliation. But this woman in whose veins flowed the blood of Rahab as well as Jezebel had a rich history. Her people had developed a great civilization that was lost through conquest, conquered by the Hyksos, was later plagued by wars and the eventual conquest of Israelites, who came in with their own God, Yahweh. By the time the Canaanite woman approaches Jesus, she is a stranger in her own land. She is a member of a defeated race, whose culture and place in history have been lost. They are now outcasts.

For her to approach Jesus and risk humiliation is a testament to the urgency of the situation—a demon-possessed child placed her in Jesus' path. Theologically, however, it was an opportune time. Jesus had just given his disciples a charge to perform miracles only for the "lost sheep of Israel," and he was confronted with a Gentile who wanted a blessing. She was not "a lost sheep of Israel"; she was the age-old enemy of "his people." However, somewhere in God's plan for salvation, the question had to be raised: What about all the others?

Jesus could not cling to the racism of the past and the animosities of the current time of the Jewish people. The message had to be made clear that all were welcome to participate in the "realm of God on earth, as it was in heaven." The demon-possessed daughter had to be healed by the One who had healed so many. How could he not heal this child? Was ethnicity enough to stop him from performing the work that God had preordained for him to perform?

The answer after much procrastination was "No." Jesus had to open his spiritual window wider on a human world divided by race, ethnicity, religion, and doctrine and perform a divine act. Thus, the Canaanite woman's presence was more than just a story about her faith. It was a realization that God had an expansive plan for blessings and salvation that far exceeded the mission that had been articulated up to that point.

Justice Reading Strategy: The Canaanite Woman, One of Many "Foreign" Women of Faith

Jesus and the disciples were presented with the picture of salvation that God had painted long before this moment. An inclusive God had called Israel into being and gave it a designation as a chosen people while also opening the arch of salvation to "foreigners." The Hebrew people were a people defined by faith in the one God—Yahweh—not by their exclusion of other peoples. Abraham's firstborn child was born of an Egyptian woman, Hagar. The Hebrews' first convert into Judaism in the promised land was a Canaanite woman, Rahab. When the Queen of Sheba visited Solomon, she praised his God and earned the right to sit in judgment of the Pharisees in the end time. Moses' first wife was a Midianite and his adopted mother, an Egyptian. Thus, God did not mean for this story to be only for the "lost sheep of Israel." This salvation history would continue to be for all who have faith.

It took this bold and audacious Canaanite woman to bring the salvation story back into the realm of what God had planned. At the moment that he healed her daughter, Jesus authenticated his divine status. He came as the Son of God to act on behalf of the sins of all, Jew and Gentile alike.

The role that this woman played in the salvation history of God is pivotal to the message that is to be conveyed by Jesus' ministry. The gospel, the good news, is for all. Somehow this woman, an outcast in society, a woman born into second-class citizenship, knows that there is an answer somewhere, and then she encounters Jesus. Her perseverance brings out the most important message of the gospel.

Conclusion

This part of the book has attempted to present the virtue of perseverance within the context of the Gospel's story about the Canaanite (Syrophoenician) woman who approached Jesus for a miracle. A man who performed many miracles in the past tried to walk away from this woman without granting her plea for her daughter. In order to make certain that the mandates of Jesus about children, about the faithful, and about women continue to resonate as the major themes in his ministry, the question had to be raised, What is Jesus doing in this scripture?

While the answers to the question might vary, the end result is what really counts. Jesus, a divine man in a human body, reached beyond ethnicity, classism, and hatred and healed a demon-possessed child because of the persistence and perseverance of a mother who would not let him go until she got a blessing for her child. This is indeed a story about more than the faith of this woman. It is a story about Jesus and the remarkable legacy of his ministry. Jesus did not pass her by; he gave her a blessing.

Reflecting on the Canaanite Woman

This chapter includes questions for reflection on the Canaanite woman's story and scriptural references for the virtue of perseverance. These questions can be used as a part of a group Bible study, or they can be used as an opportunity to grow in personal spiritual development.

Reflection on the Canaanite Woman and Perseverance

The following biblical references to perseverance can be used for further biblical reflection on perseverance as a virtue and as a requirement for Christian community. In addition, these scriptures can be used as a means of personal ethical guidance and as a way of increasing your understanding of the Bible.

1. The following passages reflect upon how God keeps us strong in our faith. Read them for discussion and reflection.

Psalm 37:24
Psalm 121:3–8
Psalm 145:20

John 6:37
Romans 8:35–39

2. God's admonishment not to abandon our faith can be found in these scriptural references.

1 Timothy 1:19–20
1 Timothy 6:20–21
2 Timothy 2:17–18
Hebrews 3:16–18

3. When you read the story of the Canaanite woman, what message do you get from her determination and perseverance, even in the midst of humiliation?

4. Reflect upon Jesus' reaction to the Canaanite woman. What is your assessment of why he responded in this manner?

5. In your own faith journey, where do you feel that you had to persevere in order to reap the blessings that God had in store for you?

Conclusion

> For the moment suffice it to say that understanding ourselves to
> be in covenant with other people involves believing that we and
> they belong to the same moral community; that in this commu-
> nity each person matters in his or her own right and not merely
> as something useful to the society; that we all participate in the
> moral community by entrusting ourselves to others and in turn
> by accepting their entrusting; and that in the moral community
> each of us has enduring responsibility to all the others.[1]

As *Daughters of Dignity* has tried to point out, the development of moral
communities has always had a valued place in the tradition of African
Americans. For many, it was structured around the means of survival for
a community of people. This conclusion provides a small sampling of
resources to assist churches in envisioning new ways to create moral and
ethical communities for African American women of faith. *Daughters of
Dignity* has looked at the faith history of African American women in
the centuries leading up to the present. In so doing, the book has also
attempted to broaden the perspective of African American women of
faith by looking at African biblical women who have exhibited the

virtues of justice, love, faith, wisdom, and perseverance. It is hoped that by bringing together the lives of African American women with those of African biblical women, a useful resource has been developed.

More specifically in this conclusion, the intent is to look at ways that this information and these new reading strategies might be used to strengthen women's ministries, Bible studies, and personal spiritual growth and development. To this end, this conclusion offers three exercises that flow from the four objectives set out in the beginning of the book. Within each of these four areas, there are opportunities for the reader to use the book to initiate and reenvision innovative ministries.

The four objectives identified in the introduction to the book are (1) developing new insights into Christian virtues; (2) creating ministries designed to reclaim Christian virtues for contemporary women; (3) exploring new approaches to personal spiritual growth; and (4) employing new reading strategies for the Bible.

EXERCISE 1.
Objective: To Develop New Insights into Christian Virtues

Daughters of Dignity is formatted in five parts; each part identifies a specific virtue. Each part introduces one African American woman whose writings, speeches, or life exemplified the particular virtue. It provides scriptures and retells the story of an African biblical woman who personified the virtue as she participated in God's salvific plan for humanity. Some prominent traditional interpretations of the text are presented along with an introduction to the justice reading strategy that broadens the scope of the interpretation to include a more holistic reading of the scripture.

This process can be repeated in your women's Bible study. Using the information given here about three African American women, do the following:

1. Identify the virtue that each woman exemplifies, given the information provided.
2. Identify a biblical woman who also exhibits that virtue.
3. Select the scriptural references that provide the narrative about the biblical woman.

4. Invite Bible study participants to retell the story in their own words.
5. Discuss the ways in which the biblical woman exemplifies the virtue.
6. Return to the African American woman and relate her story to that of the biblical woman.
7. Encourage the Bible study group to create a short speech, homily, or play that brings together the story of each woman with an emphasis on how the virtue identified is relevant to today's women.
8. Write a letter to the worship committee of the church or the pastor, and propose a sermon on the biblical woman identified, with an emphasis on how this woman fits into God's plan for salvation.
9. Rewrite the story so that it might be read to a children's church school class.
10. Develop a rites-of-passage ministry for young women that would include a core set of virtues for a young girl transitioning into womanhood.

Voices of Virtue: Using the Lives of African American Women to Stress the Virtues of Womanhood

The following African American women have made significant contributions to what can be called the ethics of black womanhood. Using their brief stories, how would you incorporate them into your women's ministries as a way of strengthening the understanding of what it means to be a black woman in the twenty-first century? For example, are there biblical women whom you can relate to these women—a woman such as Deborah the judge related to Shirley Chisholm—and the courage that each exhibited?

Politics. Shirley Chisholm (1924–) was the first African American woman to be elected to the U.S. Congress. With the slogan "Unbossed and Unbought," she beat the odds in New York politics and won a seat in its twelfth congressional district. She served in Congress from 1969 to 1982, retiring from office after having reached significant milestones in U.S. history. She was the first African American to run a credible primary race for the U.S. presidency. She championed the causes of minorities, women, and the disenfranchised. She spoke out against the war in Vietnam and spoke up for the rights of the poor. She was a voice heard round the world and a political personage known for her courageous stands on issues of conscience. Her courage in most instances was not undergirded by full support from her male colleagues in the congressional black caucus nor was it buoyed by the burgeoning feminist movement. Chisholm was alone in many of her battles, but with the courage that came from a fervently religious upbringing and a keen mind, she became a symbol of integrity and courage in the political process.

In this excerpt from Chisholm's 1972 speech announcing her Presidential candidacy, what virtue would you say she exhibits most?

I am not the candidate of the women's movement of this country, although I am a woman, and I am equally proud of that. I am not the candidate of any political bosses or special interests. . . . I am the candidate of the people.

We must turn away from the control of the prosaic, the privileged, and the old line, tired politicians to open our society to the energies and abilities of countless new groups of Americans—women, blacks, browns, Indians, Orientals and youth—so that they can develop their own full potential and thereby participate equally and enthusiastically in building a strong and just society, rich in its diversity and noble in its quality of life. . . . I stand here without the endorsements of any big-name politicians or celebrities.[2]

In 1993, discussing the new leadership in the 103rd Congress, Shirley Chisholm, now retired, spoke about her assessment of the current political leadership. What virtue do you believe is best exhibited in this excerpt from that interview?

Something I am hearing. Something that really makes me feel very good. Both blacks and whites, old and young, rich and poor say over and over again, in their own way of putting it, they want the truth. Even if the truth hurts, they cannot stand to have hypocrisy and the double and triple standards that sometimes appear to emanate from Washington, D.C., out here to the people all over the country and then later find out that it was just a cover up. . . . I happen to feel that we do not have the same kind of concern, commitment, courage and resiliency in much of the black leadership today as we had in the days of old. There's something missing and it has nothing to do with ability. But there's a certain kind of courage that I do not see in black leaders today like I saw in the leaders of yore.[3]

Ministry. Florence Spearing Randolph (1866–1951) was one of the first women to be ordained in the African Methodist Episcopal Zion Church. This is an excerpt from a sermon that she gave on hope, using as her text 1 Corinthians 13:13.

We must work unitedly, for united efforts bring great victories. We must not be contented simply to build churches, we must build race institutions of every kind and endeavor to support them independently. If there is one above another needed in these northern states it is a home of protection for girls. Believing that God helps those who help themselves, and being encouraged by hope; we are about to start a work that we believe to be one of the needs of the race, namely to establish in Jersey City, an industrial Christian home for colored girls where the unfortunate Afro-American girl can start life anew; where the heart can be taught the pure love of God, the mind to think and the hand to work. Many a well desiring girl has gone further and further into vice and degradation in the hour of temptation, for the want of a single Christian friend. This is indeed a serious thought and should sink deep into the heart of every woman.

Are we looking forward to the next generation for a better condition of affairs? Then something must be done for the protection and elevation of our girls, for they are the future mothers, under their care will be reared the future men and women, who must fill the places of those who are now on the stage of action.[4]

Florence Spearing Randolph was one of the few women to pastor a number of churches in the African Methodist Episcopal Zion Church. Though labeled insane by her husband and family, Randolph proceeded to answer her call to the ministry and was willing to give up her husband and family in order to follow her call from God. Her determination to be ordained sparked a raucous debate among the ministers and bishops in the New Jersey Conference of the A.M.E. Church. Eventually, Randolph was ordained a deacon in 1903. Two years earlier she had represented the church in a conference in Europe and received attention because of her preaching and lecturing. Her largely unpaid pastoral assignments were in the New Jersey and New York Conferences.

Randolph represented the kind of faith and perseverance that other African American women in the ministry possessed. She put that faith to work in the pulpit, and she moved beyond it and began working for social justice in the community, particularly as it related to instilling the virtues of womanhood into young women.

These are a few of the voices of African American women who spoke out for the virtues of African American womanhood as an avocation, but who also served as exemplars of those virtues in their dedication and commitment to the uplift of black people. It was an intentional effort on their part, and it was a continuous effort to bring about the dignity that had been stifled in many circumstances and destroyed in others. Use these stories and more as you strengthen your women's ministries around the virtues of womanhood.

EXERCISE 2.

Objective: To Create Ministries Designed to Reclaim Christian Virtues for Contemporary Women

There are many areas in which African American women are attacked by the media and portrayed in a bad light. For African American women of many different classes and backgrounds, the problem is the same. If the church is to reclaim its place as a champion of positive Christian virtues for African American women, it will have to deal with the media. The portrayal of black women in newspapers, on television, and in music is much more derogatory today than it has ever been. If the church decides to be proactive with its ministries, some questioning of the media will have to take place.

These scenarios are followed by reflection questions that might help women's ministries to develop proactive responses to local media portrayal of black women. Women's ministries might want to start awareness campaigns and encourage congregations to respond verbally and economically when negative images are presented.

African American Women Stereotyped as Being on Welfare, Lazy, and Promiscuous. This book began with a description of a *Washington Post* article about a welfare mother and her daughter. Now that you have read about the virtues of womanhood, revisit that scenario and explore ways to be proactive in your own community about negative images of African American women.

On the front page of the Sunday, October 19, 1997, issue of the *Washington Post,* there appeared a young African American woman, age fifteen, sitting on a sofa with her thumb in her mouth, her hair uncombed, wearing a T-shirt, with a nine-month-old baby hanging between her legs. The caption read: "Generations of Pain: Denise Jordan Is Off Welfare and Loves Her Job. But What About Her Daughter?"

The facts: The U.S. Census Bureau in 1994 counted 25.4 million poor whites and 10 million poor African Americans. There are more white women than black women on welfare. Nearly twice as many white as black children are growing up in poverty. In the November 8, 1997, edition of the *Washington Post,* Jesse Jackson was quoted as saying that "the media stereotypes black Americans as a race of losers and misfits. A black mask has been put on the face of poverty. We must whiten the face of poverty to change the dynamics of the debate."

1. What are some of the issues involved in this type of portrayal of black women?
2. What solutions or proactive steps would you consider taking regarding this type of media coverage?
3. What long-term solutions do you see in addressing young women who find themselves in the same position as this young woman?

4. How would you describe the image of black women in your local media?
5. Teenage pregnancy is an issue. What strategies can the church employ to bring about change or reform?
6. Is it your belief that the images put forth about black women have an impact only on poor women, or are all African American women judged by the same standards?

African American Women in Leadership and the Media. In 1994, Carol Moseley-Braun, the only African American woman to serve in the U.S. Senate, was ridiculed by some members of the congressional press gallery in the following manner. They placed a newspaper photograph of the senator and the former president of Haiti, Jean Bertrand Aristide, on a sheet of paper. Underneath the photograph a handwritten note asked people to write a caption for the picture. Sexist and racist remarks were written on the paper as it hung in the press gallery for all to see. Two black reporters had the sign removed.

1. Why do you think that at the highest level of achievement, black women continue to experience humiliating situations based upon their race?
2. What kind of proactive stance should black women's organizations and sororities take to fight continued humiliation of black women, no matter what their achievements?
3. Reread the scriptures about Vashti (Esther 1) and Jezebel. Are there any redeeming qualities that you can discover in the portrayal of these two women?

Media Coverage of Positive Events Affecting African American Women. The Million Woman March in 1997 resulted in approximately 1.5 million African American women assembling in Philadelphia. The city businesses are said to have made more than $100 million that weekend.

1. The Million Woman March did not draw any national black leaders as the large assemblage of African American women converged on the city of Philadelphia. Why do you think this was the case?
2. With such a positive outpouring of black women, why do you believe the media provided so little coverage?

3. One of the recommendations from the march was that black women begin establishing rites-of-passage programs for young women so that values can be passed on from one generation to another. Is this a recommendation that you agree with? If so, why? If not, why not?

African American Women and Rap Music. Young African American women are constantly bombarded by music lyrics that offend and defame them. Dr. C. Delores Tucker, of the National Black Women's Political Caucus, was one of a few African American leaders who actively challenged the music industry. She sued the record companies, testified against the industry before Congress, and actively campaigned for change in the images and use of black women in music videos and lyrics.

1. Do you know of other leaders in your community who have been vocal about the music industry and black women?
2. Is your church equipped to provide support for a ministry that would redirect the interest, energy, and aspirations of young women who are attracted to a music culture that attempts to degrade them? If so, explain. If not, how would you suggest that the church get involved in solving the problem?

EXERCISE 3.

Objectives 3 and 4: To Develop New Insights into Personal Spiritual Growth and to Employ New Reading Strategies for the Bible

There are a number of ways that African American women can expand their own spiritual development and growth. One is by reading some of the African American women theologians who have written books that specifically address the issues facing black women. The following summaries of three such books should be a helpful starting point for creating new reading strategies that will enhance spiritual growth and development.

Jacquelyn Grant

Key work: Jacquelyn Grant, *White Women's Christ and Black Women's Jesus: Feminist Christology and Womanist Response* (Atlanta: Scholars Press, 1989).

Dr. Jacquelyn Grant is a professor of systematic theology at the Interdenominational Theological Center, Atlanta, Georgia. She holds a B.A. from Bennett College, a master's of divinity from the Interdenominational Theological Center, and a Ph.D. from Union Theological Seminary in New York. The African Methodist Episcopal Church scholar is noted for making critical distinctions between black women's and white women's theological interpretations of Scripture and faith.

> In this work I argue that feminist theology suffers from the same problem as the nineteenth-century feminist movement—that is, it is a single issue movement; its issue is sexism. As such, it could not possibly address adequately the reality of non-White women in general, and Black women in particular.
>
> Racism/sexism/classism as a corporate point of departure for doing theology and Christology is embraced as an appropriate and corrective approach in theology. This tri-dimensional analysis is more consistent with the way Jesus identified the Christ. . . . The basic contention here, then, is that the Christ is more likely to be found in the community of Black women.[5]

Grant systematically sets forth the case for the unique manner in which African American women view the Bible and think about and experience God. She presents the conditions for establishing a theology for African American women known as womanist theology, which is distinct from that of feminist. In actuality, her theological claims for womanist theology are more universal than those of feminists in that they go beyond the context of sexism and patriarchy. Grant criticizes feminist theology as racist—claiming that in its preoccupation with patriarchy, it overlooks issues facing women of color. Black women's issues are inextricably bound by color, economic standing, and gender. Therefore, Grant concludes that womanist theology is concerned with race, class, and gender. Using the lives of black women in the United States and placing them next to the belief that there is a biblical preference for poor and oppressed persons, Grant makes the case for the development of a theology that speaks to black women's experience.

By participating in the dialogue and discussion regarding their unique faith stories, black women are engaging in the process for liberation that will have a direct impact on their lives. This, Grant believes, is not available to them with the same degree of depth and fullness in white feminist theology.

After making the case for the establishment of womanist theology, Grant compares the holistic definition of womanist theology with the partial definition of feminist theology. The latter she refers to as only partially liberating. Grant maintains that feminist theology, as defined and as operative, is currently racist and classist.

Using the experiences of slavery and black women's experience with domestic service, she formulates a theology that encompasses the point at which oppression is reflected in the intersection of race, gender, and class. At this point Grant borrows the term "womanist," created by author Alice Walker, to describe the uniqueness of black women's faith tradition and belief system.

Because it is important to distinguish black and white women's experiences, it is also important to note these differences in the way they might read and interpret the biblical stories. For example, if both were reading the Hagar and Sarah story, black women would most likely identify with Hagar, and white women might identify readily with Sarah. Two different reading strategies produce two different ways of interpreting the story. Grant writes, "I maintain that Black women scholars should follow Alice Walker by describing our theological activity as 'womanist theology.' The term womanist refers to Black women's experiences. It accents, as Walker says, our being responsible, in charge, outrageous, courageous and audacious enough to demand the right to think theologically and to do it independently of both White and Black men and White women."[6]

With these words, Grant injects into the lexicon womanist theology, a term that continues to evolve as a definition for the theological claims of African American women and other women of color. In putting forth the womanist criticism of white feminist theology, Grant also challenges black women not to discount the works of feminists, but to build on them.

Dr. Jacquelyn Grant is considered one of the trailblazers in the womanist theological movements as well as the first to coin the term "womanist theology," under which more than two dozen womanist scholars have begun to explore the ramifications of sexism, racism, and classism in the lives and spiritual growth and development of women of color. Each of these women introduces a different reading strategy for black women so that they might get a more holistic understanding of the Scriptures.

Katie G. Cannon

Key work: Katie G. Cannon, *Black Womanist Ethics* (Atlanta: Scholars Press, 1988).

Katie Cannon, professor of Christian ethics at Temple University, Philadelphia, holds a B.S. degree from Barber Scotia College, a master's of divinity from Interdenominational Theological Center in Atlanta, and a Ph.D. from Union Theological Seminary in New York. The Presbyterian scholar developed the concept of black womanist ethics in her 1988 publication of the same name. Cannon explores the moral condition of African American women, setting the foundation for the establishment of a womanist ethic using as resources the works of novelist and anthropologist Zora Neale Hurston and theologians Howard Thurman and Martin Luther King Jr.

For Cannon, the major question emerged as she attempted to relate "the Christian doctrines preached in the Black Church to the suffering, oppression and exploitation of Black people in the society. How could Christians—who were white—flatly and openly, refuse to treat as fellow human beings, Christians who had African ancestry? Was not the essence of the Gospel mandate a call to eradicate affliction, despair and systems of injustice?"[7]

Cannon's response to these questions led her to recognize that the ethics and claims of Protestantism were not applicable to African Americans because the underlying assumptions for white Protestants were not available to blacks. Thus, even though blacks exhibited these traits, the results of their actions would not necessarily be the same.

For example, dominant ethics makes a virtue of qualities that lead to economic success—self-reliance, frugality and industry. These qualities are based on an assumption that success is possible for anyone who tries. . . . Racism does not allow Black women and Black men to labor habitually in beneficial work with the hope of saving expenses by avoiding waste so that they can develop a standard of living that is congruent with the American ideal. . . . Theoretical and analytical analyses demonstrate that to embrace work as a "moral essential" means that Black women are still the last hired to do the work which white men, white women and men of color refuse to do, and at a wage which men and white women refuse to accept. Black women, placed in jobs that have proven to be detrimental to their health, are doing the most menial, tedious and by far the most underpaid work, if they manage to get a job at all.[8]

What Cannon attempts to do in this book, then, is to construct an ethic that applies to the lived experience of black women, using as a foundation their historical moral experience as depicted in the literature of one of the most prolific black women writers, Zora Neale Hurston. Cannon looks at the elements of a paradigm that can be compared and contrasted with theological principles and ethics. She cautions, however, that the ethic that emerges must lead toward liberation and away from oppression. To this extent she proposes that the ethic that emerges is not the one that holds the same assumptions, or the same tenets, as the Anglo-Protestant American tradition.

In developing this ethic, Cannon first does a historical analysis of the moral structure of black women's lives and then looks at the literature as reflected in the writings of Hurston to come up with a framework for an ethic for black women:

My goal is not to arrive at my own perspective or normative ethic. Rather, what I am pursuing is an investigation (a) that will help Black women, and others who care, to understand and to appreciate the richness of their own moral struggle through the life of the common people and the oral tradition; (b) to further understandings of some of the differences between ethics of life under oppression and established moral approaches which take for granted freedom and a wide range of choices. I am being suggestive of one possible ethical approach, not exhaustive.[9]

Cannon proceeds to use the works of Hurston to extract ethical considerations for black women. She then moves to the more traditional theological resources of Howard Thurman and Martin Luther King Jr. Although neither King nor Thurman dealt specifically with the oppression of black women, Cannon employs their analysis of the condition of black oppression in general to pattern a black womanist ethic.

This book, which emerged as a result of Cannon's dissertation, is a foundational document for the continued work of womanist ethics because it seeks to give a response to the lived realities of black women. Equally important, Cannon challenges the black church and the external society to respond to these issues. She notes that even though both King and Thurman treat the evils of racism and classism, neither attacks sexism as a part of that evil. Nevertheless, she still finds their criticisms and analyses useful resources for developing a strong womanist ethics.

Emilie M. Townes

Key work: Emilie M. Townes, *In a Blaze of Glory: Womanist Spirituality as Social Witness* (Nashville: Abingdon Press, 1995).

Apocalyptic vision. Eschatological hope. These twin concepts move within womanist spirituality. The apocalyptic vision evolves from crisis and martyrdom. It is a theo-ethical, sociopolitical manifesto that refuses to accept or tolerate injustice. It seeks to overcome the discrepancy (and attendant craziness) between what is and what should be—the discrepancy between empirical reality and legitimate expectations. Apocalyptic vision in womanist work and thought speaks prophecy and cautions the pyramidic towers of evil to beware.[10]

Dr. Emilie M. Townes is a professor of Christian ethics at Union Theological Seminary in New York City. She received three degrees from the University of Chicago—a bachelor of arts (1977), a master of arts (1979), and a doctor of ministry (1982). In 1989 she received a Ph.D. in Christian ethics from Northwestern. Townes is one of the early trail-blazers who contributed to the definition of womanist theology. In her book *In a Blaze of Glory,* the Christian ethicist seeks out a more holistic approach to womanist Christian ethics, calling for the full incorporation of love, justice, and righteousness in the quest for a more socially accountable womanist theology.

Townes defines the womanist hermeneutic using four areas, giving proof of its social witness, its historical foundation, and its spiritual testimony as evidenced in the lives of black women in America from the advent of slavery to the contemporary period.

As she moves from the historical look at African American spirituality—the blend of West African spirituality and Christianity—she chronicles the impact of eighteenth- and nineteenth-century social justice movements of black women and their attempts at developing a womanhood of faith. In the remainder of the book, Townes uses literature to address the womanist ethics associated with the understanding of such things as the nature of lynching from within the black community (neoconservatism) and from without the black community (environmental racism). The latter is a new area of emphasis for womanist theologians and ethicists, which has the potential for exerting a significant influence on discussions about womanist theology. Using Alice Walker and Paule Marshall novels, Townes addresses the issues of the power of cultural images and self-esteem, respectively.

One particular area of cultural courage in interpretative hermeneutics can be found in Townes's focus on the black middle class. In a pioneering critique of the social consciousness of the black middle class, Townes defines a Christian social ethic for African Americans caught in the midst of progress, racism, and classism. She addresses the ethics of middle-class black women and their obligation to move beyond guilt from success to action for oppressed blacks left behind. In this respect she offers an ethics of accountability that is rooted in communal life and in the history of black women.

African Americans must take this into the communal context. Our self-respect, our self-esteem, our sense of self—individually and collectively—are under assault. Colorism points to the fact that we must be concerned about what we do to ourselves and how we respond to the structural injustices. As people of faith, our spirituality must be rich enough to help us gain clarity as to why and how we allow colorism and caste to have such a strong impact on how we see the range of hues that make up the African American community. Such a spirituality will guide us into a witness that helps us decide how we are going to love ourselves and one another rather than rely on popular culture, even our own popular culture, to tell us who we have been, who we are, and where we are heading, and how we are to behave with one another in justice and hope.[11]

Finally, Townes poses the question that undergirds all of these inquiries, which is: "Do we want to be healed?" She answers it with a resounding "Yes!" For Townes, the response to this question does not lie within the context of a separate force labeled "spirituality," but it is integrated into the fabric, the life, the humanity, the vision, and the hope of the oppressed. It is the wellspring from which love, justice, and righteousness find sustenance, and it is the essence of the faith tradition that is given voice by womanist theologians and ethicists.

Conclusion

African American women have made tremendous strides from the time they came to America as slaves in the bottom of slave ships. They have been able to turn a situation destined for dehumanization into a triumph of the will and the spirit by a boundless faith and a persistent and conscious hope. Yet now in the twenty-first century, there are still concerns that stem from a need to reinforce some of the tenets of earlier days. Black women still are disproportionately represented in the AIDS population, in teenage pregnancies, in poverty, and in single parentage. Black women still are economically behind in salaries and in wages. African American women are still suffering disproportionately from health care issues that cause earlier deaths and more stressful lives than other women. Yet the indomitable spirit of black women has permitted them to soar to great heights past major obstacles. This paradoxical existence calls even more for African American women to be diligent about their quest for dignity in the midst of attempted degradation. In the midst of a moral decline, African American women have a history that allows them to lead a reformation not only for African Americans, but also for other people in the world.

Daughters of Dignity has been an attempt to bring together the historical, religious, and ethical foundation upon which such a reformation can occur in the twenty-first century. Hopefully, African American women will continue to build new visions and strong families through faithful witness.

Notes

Introduction

1. Madeleine Burnside, *Spirit of the Passage: The Transatlantic Slave Trade in the Seventeenth Century,* ed. Rosemarie Robotham (New York: Simon & Schuster, 1997), 131–32.

2. Ibid., 161.

3. Darlene Clark Hines, Elsa Barkley Brown, and Rosalyn Terborg-Penn, eds., *Black Women in America: An Historical Encyclopedia,* vol. I (Bloomington: Indiana University Press, 1993), 8.

4. Carrie Meek, official taped proceedings of Congressional Black Caucus Legislative Weekend, 103rd Congress, September 1993, as they appeared in *African American Women in Congress: Forming and Transforming History,* by LaVerne M. Gill (New Brunswick, N.J.: Rutgers University Press, 1997), 190.

5. Renita Weems, "Reading Her Way through the Struggle: African American Women and the Bible," in *Stony the Road We Trod: African American Biblical Interpretation,* ed. Cain Hope Felder (Minneapolis: Fortress Press, 1991), 60–72.

6. Renita Weems, *Just a Sister Away: A Womanist Vision of Women's Relationships in the Bible* (San Diego: LuraMedia, 1988), viii.

7. Julianne Malveaux, ed., *Voices of Vision: African American Women on the Issues* (Washington, D.C.: National Council of Negro Women, 1996), 309–12.

8. Hines et al., *Black Women in America,* vol. II, 1309.

9. Vincent Harding, foreword to *Jesus and the Disinherited,* by Howard Thurman (Boston: Beacon Press, 1996), page unnumbered.

10. Ibid., 20.

11. Toni Morrison, *Beloved* (New York: Random House, 1987).

12. Van A. Harvey, *A Handbook of Theological Terms* (New York: Collier Books, 1964), 248–49.

13. Ibid.

14. Cain Hope Felder, "The Bible, Black Women and Ministry," *Journal of Religious Thought* 41:2 (fall–winter 1984–85): 48.

15. Ibid.

16. Cain Hope Felder, *Troubling Biblical Waters: Race, Class and Family* (Maryknoll, N.Y.: Orbis Books, 1989).

17. Felder, *Stony the Road We Trod.*

1. Justice as a Virtue and Rosa Parks

1. Harvey, *A Handbook of Theological Terms,* 134.

2. Peter Singer, ed., *A Companion to Ethics* (Oxford, U.K.: Blackwell Publishers, 1993), 33.

3. Harvey, *A Handbook of Theological Terms,* 369.

4. Wayne G. Boulton, Thomas D. Kennedy, and Allen Verhey, eds., *From Christ to the World: Introductory Readings in Christian Ethics* (Grand Rapids, Mich.: Eerdmans, 1994), 235.

5. Martin Luther King Jr., excerpts from "Nonviolence and Racial Justice," in "Christian Century," in *A Testament of Hope: The Essential Writings and Speeches of Martin Luther King, Jr.,* ed. James Melvin Washington (San Francisco: HarperSanFrancisco, 1986), 9.

6. Rita Dove, *On the Bus with Rosa Parks* (New York: Norton, 1999), 81.

7. Hines et al., *Black Women in America,* vol. II, 559.

8. Ibid., 908.

2. The Story of Hagar: God's Blueprint for Justice

1. Henry Louis Gates, general ed., *Six Women's Slave Narratives* (New York: Oxford University Press, 1988), 3.

2. Delores S. Williams, *Sisters in the Wilderness: The Challenge of Womanist God-Talk* (New York: Orbis Books, 1994), v.

3. Weems, *Just a Sister Away.*

4. Hammurabi (ca. 1728–1686 B.C.E.) was the ruler of Mesopotamia, the land that Abraham left to go to Palestine/Syria or Canaan.

5. John W. Waters, "Who Was Hagar?" in *Stony the Road We Trod,* 199.

6. Ibid., 192.

7. Williams, *Sisters in the Wilderness,* 7–8.

8. Ibid., 8–9.

9. Ibid., 6.

10. Rosamond and James Weldon Johnson, "Lift Every Voice and Sing," 1921.

11. Bernhard W. Anderson, *Understanding the Old Testament,* 4th ed. (Englewood Cliffs, N.J.: Prentice Hall, 1986), 34.

12. William M. Brimner, trans., *The History of al-Tabari, vol. 2, Prophets and Patriarchs* (New York: State University of New York Press, 1987), vii. Note: The United Nations' UNESCO included the translation of al-Tabari's History in its Collection of Representative Works. This translation is the result of that decision. The translation project was underwritten in part by the National Endowment for the Humanities in the United States.

13. Ibid., 64.

14. Ibid., 65.

15. Ibid., 68.

16. Ibid., 70.

17. Ibid., 70–71.

18. Ibid., 72.

4. Love as a Virtue and Osceola McCarty

1. Washington, *A Testament of Hope*, 16.

2. Ibid.

3. Ibid., 19.

4. William L. Reese, ed., *Dictionary of Philosophy and Religion* (Amherst, N.Y.: Prometheus Press, 1996), 427–28.

5. Osceola McCarty, *Simple Wisdom for Rich Living* (Marietta, Ga.: Longstreet Press, 1996), 75.

6. Ibid.

5. The Story of Zipporah: A Peculiar Woman in Salvation History

1. Zora Neale Hurston, *Moses, Man of the Mountain: A Novel* (New York: HarperPerennial, 1991), 102.

2. Steven Spielberg, producer, *Prince of Egypt*, DreamWorks Productions, Hollywood, California, 1998.

3. Anderson, *Understanding the Old Testament*, 52.

4. Jeremiah Wright, *Africans Who Shaped Our Faith* (Chicago: Urban Ministries, 1995), 81.

5. F. B. Meyer, *Devotional Commentary on Exodus* (Grand Rapids, Mich.: Kregel Publications, 1978), 80.

6. W. H. Gispen, *Bible Student's Commentary: Exodus*, trans. Ed van der Maas (Grand Rapids, Mich.: Zondervan, 1982), 64.

7. Wright, *Africans Who Shaped Our Faith*, 99.

7. Faith as a Virtue and Sojourner Truth

1. Reese, *Dictionary of Philosophy and Religion*, 222.

2. Nell Irvin Painter, *Sojourner Truth: A Life, a Symbol* (New York: Norton, 1996), 73.

3. Nell Irvin Painter, "Sojourner Truth (c. 1799–1883)," in *Black Women in America,* vol. II, 1172–76.

4. Ibid., 1176.

8. The Story of Rahab: From Prostitute to Ancestor of Jesus

1. John Calvin, *Commentaries on the Book of Joshua,* trans. Henry Beveridge (Grand Rapids, Mich.: Eerdmans, 1949), 45–46.

2. Richard D. Nelson, *Joshua: A Commentary,* The Old Testament Library (Louisville: Westminster John Knox, 1997), 36–40.

3. Ibid., 42–43.

4. Ibid., 43.

10. Wisdom as a Virtue and Mary McLeod Bethune

1. John R. Kohlenberger III, *The NRSV Concordance, Unabridged* (Grand Rapids, Mich.: Zondervan, 1991), 73.

2. Harvey, *A Handbook of Theological Terms,* 252.

3. The Hebrew word Labab can be translated as either "mind" or "heart." Translations vary as to which term is used.

4. James L. Kugel, "Introduction to Psalms and Wisdom," in *Harper's Bible Commentary,* ed. James L. Mays (San Francisco: Harper & Row, 1988), 398.

5. Malveaux, *Voices of Vision,* 309–12.

6. Hines et al., *Black Women in America,* vol. I, 113–26.

7. Cain Hope Felder, general ed., *The Original African Heritage Study Bible* (Nashville: James C. Winston Publishing Co., 1993), 942.

11. The Story of the Queen of Sheba: A Queen's Search for Faith and Wisdom

1. Felder, *Troubling Biblical Waters,* 30.

2. Gill, *African American Women in Congress,* 25.

3. Bettye Collier-Thomas, *Daughters of Thunder: Black Women Preachers and Their Sermons, 1850–1979* (San Francisco: Jossey-Bass, 1998), 123, 101.

4. The *Kebra Nagast* (Glory of Kings) is the Ethiopian book of national, religious, and cultural history that tells the story about the dynastic leadership of Ethiopia stemming from the union between Queen Makeda (Queen of Sheba) and King Solomon. It is a book of national, cultural, and religious importance to the Ethiopian people.

5. Miguel F. Brooks, ed., *Kebra Nagast English: A Modern Translation: The Glory of Kings* (Lawrenceville, N.J.: Red Sea Press, 1996), 22.

6. Jacob Lassner, *Demonizing the Queen of Sheba: Boundaries of Gender and Culture in Post Biblical Judaism and Medieval Islam* (Chicago: University of Chicago Press, 1993), 162.

7. Ibid., 168–69.

8. Ibid., 1.

9. Josephus Flavius, *The Complete Works of Josephus Flavius,* trans. William Winston (Grand Rapids, Mich.: Kregel Publications, 1981), 180.

10. Frank M. Snowden Jr., *Blacks in Antiquity: Ethiopians in the Greco-Roman Experience* (Cambridge, Mass.: Belknap Press of Harvard University Press, 1970), 114.

11. George Arthur Buttrick, commentary ed., *The Interpreter's Bible,* vol. 8 (Nashville: Abingdon Press, 1994), 212.

12. John Calvin, *Commentary on a Harmony of the Evangelists, Matthew, Mark, and Luke* (Grand Rapids, Mich.: Eerdmans, 1949), 96.

13. Paul J. Achtemeier, general ed., *Harper's Bible Dictionary* (San Francisco: Harper & Row, 1985), 920.

14. Snowden, *Blacks in Antiquity,* 202–3.

15. Ibid.

16. Paul R. House, *The New American Commentary,* vol. 8, 1, 2 Kings (Nashville: Broadman Holman, 1995), 161.

17. Brooks, *Kebra Nagast English,* 21.

18. Ibid., 22–23.

19. Ibid., 23.

20. Ibid., 176.

21. Ibid., 180–86.

22. Felder, *The Original African Heritage Study Bible,* 939–40.

23. Ibid., 942.

13. Perseverance as a Virtue and Fannie Lou Hamer

1. Linda Reed, "Fannie Lou Hamer (1917–1977)," in *Black Women in America,* vol. 1, 519.

14. The Story of the Canaanite Woman: A Persevering Spirit Encounters Jesus

1. Martin Bernal, *Black Athena: The Afroasiatic Roots of Classical Civilization,* vol. 1, The Fabrication of Ancient Greece (New Brunswick, N.J.: Rutgers University Press, 1987), 511.

2. Watson E. Mills and Richard Wilson, general eds., *Mercer Commentary on the Bible* (Macon, Ga.: Mercer University Press, 1995), 960.

3. Edith Deen, *All of the Women of the Bible* (New York: Harper & Row, 1955), 189.

4. Mills and Wilson, *Mercer Commentary on the Bible,* 990.

Conclusion

1. Joseph L. Allen, *Love and Conflict: A Covenantal Model of Christian Ethics* (Lanham, Md.: University Press of America, 1995), 17.

2. Gill, *African American Women in Congress,* 28.

3. Ibid., 34.

4. Collier-Thomas, *Daughters of Thunder,* 120–21.

5. Jacquelyn Grant, *White Women's Christ and Black Women's Jesus: Feminist Christology and Womanist Response* (Atlanta: Scholars Press, 1989), precis.

6. Ibid., 207.

7. Katie G. Cannon, *Black Womanist Ethics* (Atlanta: Scholars Press, 1988), 1.

8. Ibid., 2.

9. Ibid., 6.

10. Emilie M. Townes, *In a Blaze of Glory: Womanist Spirituality as Social Witness* (Nashville: Abingdon Press, 1995), 121.

11. Ibid., 119.

Bibliography

Achtemeier, Paul J., general ed. *Harper's Bible Dictionary*. San Francisco: Harper & Row, 1985.

Allen, Joseph L. *Love and Conflict: A Covenant Model of Christian Ethics*. Lanham, Md.: University Press of America, 1995.

Anderson, Bernhard W. *Understanding the Old Testament*. 4th ed. Englewood Cliffs, N.J.: Prentice Hall, 1986.

Andrews, William L., ed. *Sisters of the Spirit: Three Black Women's Autobiographies of the Nineteenth Century*. Bloomington: University of Indiana Press, 1986.

Bernal, Martin. *Black Athena: The Afroasiatic Roots of Classical Civilization*. Vol. 1, *The Fabrication of Ancient Greece*. New Brunswick, N.J.: Rutgers University Press, 1987.

Boulton, Wayne G., Thomas D. Kennedy, and Allen Verhey, eds. *From Christ to the World: Introductory Readings in Christian Ethics*. Grand Rapids, Mich.: Eerdmans, 1994.

Brimner, William M., trans. *The History of al-Tabari*. Vol. 2, *Prophets and Patriarchs*. New York: State University of New York Press, 1987.

Brooks, Miguel F., ed. *Kebra Nagast English: A Modern Translation: The Glory of Kings*. Lawrenceville, N.J.: Red Sea Press, 1996.

Budge, Sir Wallis. *Egyptian Religion*. New York: Barnes & Noble, 1994.

Burnside, Madeleine. *Spirit of the Passage: The Transatlantic Slave Trade in the Seventeenth Century*. Ed. Rosemarie Robotham. New York: Simon & Schuster, 1997.

Buttrick, George Arthur, commentary ed. *The Interpreter's Bible.* Vol. 8. Nashville: Abingdon Press, 1994.

Calvin, John. *Commentary on a Harmony of the Evangelists, Matthew, Mark, and Luke.* Grand Rapids, Mich.: Eerdmans, 1949.

———. *Commentaries on the Book of Joshua.* Trans. Henry Beveridge. Grand Rapids, Mich.: Eerdmans, 1949.

Cannon, Katie G. *Black Womanist Ethics.* Atlanta: Scholars Press, 1988.

Collier-Thomas, Bettye. *Daughters of Thunder: Black Women Preachers and Their Sermons, 1850–1979.* San Francisco: Jossey-Bass, 1998.

Davis, John J. *Moses and the Gods of Egypt: Studies in Exodus.* Grand Rapids, Mich.: Baker Book House, 1971.

Deen, Edith. *All of the Women of the Bible.* New York: Harper & Row, 1955.

Dove, Rita. *On the Bus with Rosa Parks.* New York: Norton, 1999.

Felder, Cain Hope. "The Bible, Black Women and Ministry." *Journal of Religious Thought* 41:2 (fall–winter 1984–85).

———. *Troubling Biblical Waters: Race, Class and Family.* Maryknoll, N.Y.: Orbis Books. 1989.

———, ed. *Stony the Road We Trod: African American Biblical Interpretation.* Minneapolis: Fortress Press, 1991.

———, general ed. *The Original African Heritage Study Bible.* Nashville: James C. Winston Publishing Co., 1993.

Flavius, Josephus. *The Complete Works of Josephus Flavius.* Trans. William Winston. Grand Rapids, Mich.: Kregel Publications, 1981.

Gates, Henry Louis, general ed. *Six Women's Slave Narratives.* New York: Oxford University Press, 1988.

Giddings, Paula. *When and Where I Enter: The Impact of Black Women on Race and Sex in America.* New York: Bantam Books, 1984.

Gill, LaVerne M. *African American Women in Congress: Forming and Transforming History.* New Brunswick, N.J.: Rutgers University Press, 1997.

———. *African American Women Reclaiming Christian Virtues.* Course Book for Princeton Theological Seminary Continuing Education. Princeton, N.J., 1997.

———. "Womanist Theology: An Examination of the Distinctiveness of Its Theological Claims and a Narrative Account of Its Founding Mothers." Master of divinity thesis, Princeton Theological Seminary, 1997.

Gispen, W. H. *Bible Student's Commentary: Exodus.* Trans. Ed van der Maas. Grand Rapids, Mich.: Zondervan, 1982.

Grant, Jacquelyn. *White Women's Christ and Black Women's Jesus: Feminist Christology and Womanist Response.* Atlanta: Scholars Press, 1989.

Harvey, Van A. *A Handbook of Theological Terms.* New York: Collier Books, 1964.

Hines, Darlene Clark, Elsa Barkley Brown, and Rosalyn Terborg-Penn, eds. *Black Women in America: An Historical Encyclopedia.* Vol. 2. Bloomington: Indiana University Press, 1993.

House, Paul R. *The New American Commentary.* Vol. 8, 1, 2 Kings. Nashville: Broadman Holman, 1995.

Hurston, Zora Neale. *Moses, Man of the Mountain.* New York: HarperPerennial, 1991.

Kohlenberger, John R., III. *The NRSV Concordance, Unabridged.* Grand Rapids, Mich.: Zondervan, 1991.

Lassner, Jacob. *Demonizing the Queen of Sheba: Boundaries of Gender and Culture in Post Biblical Judaism and Medieval Islam.* Chicago: University of Chicago Press, 1993.

Malveaux, Julianne, ed. *Voices of Vision: African American Women on the Issues.* Washington, D.C.: National Council of Negro Women, 1996.

Mays, James L., general ed. *Harper's Bible Commentary.* San Francisco: Harper & Row, 1988.

McCarty, Osceola. *Simple Wisdom for Rich Living.* Marietta, Ga.: Longstreet Press, 1996.

Meyer, F. B. *Devotional Commentary on Exodus.* Grand Rapids, Mich.: Kregel Publications, 1978.

Mills, Watson E., and Richard Wilson, general eds. *Mercer Commentary on the Bible.* Macon, Ga.: Mercer University Press, 1995.

Morrison, Toni. *Playing in the Dark: Whiteness and the Literary Imagination.* New York: Random House. 1992.

Nelson, Richard D. *Joshua: A Commentary.* The Old Testament Library. Louisville: Westminster John Knox, 1997.

Newsom, Carol A., and Sharon H. Ringe, eds. *The Women's Bible Commentary.* Louisville: Westminster/John Knox, 1992.

Painter, Nell Irvin. *Sojourner Truth: A Life, a Symbol.* New York: Norton, 1996.

Reese, William L., ed. *Dictionary of Philosophy and Religion.* Amherst, N.Y.: Humanities Press, 1996.

Singer, Peter, ed. *A Companion to Ethics.* Oxford, U.K.: Blackwell Publishers, 1993.

Snowden, Frank M., Jr. *Blacks in Antiquity: Ethiopians in the Greco-Roman Experience.* Cambridge, Mass.: Belknap Press of Harvard University Press, 1970.

Thurman, Howard. *Jesus and the Disinherited.* Foreword by Vincent Harding. Boston: Beacon Press, 1996.

Townes, Emilie M. *In a Blaze of Glory: Womanist Spirituality as Social Witness.* Nashville: Abingdon Press, 1995.

Washington, James M., ed. *A Testament of Hope: The Essential Writings and Speeches of Martin Luther King, Jr.* San Francisco: HarperSanFrancisco, 1986.

Weems, Renita J. *Just a Sister Away: A Womanist Vision of Women's Relationships in the Bible.* San Diego: LuraMedia, 1988.

Williams, Delores S. *Sisters in the Wilderness: The Challenge of Womanist God-Talk.* New York: Orbis Books, 1994.

Wright, Jeremiah A., Jr. *Africans Who Shaped Our Faith: A Study of 10 Biblical Personalities.* Chicago: Urban Ministries, 1995.

Index

white women, interpretations of
Scripture, 117–19
*White Women's Christ and Black
Women's Jesus* (Grant), 116–19
wife selection, and Hagar, 16, 24
Williams, Delores, 11, 12, 18–19
wisdom, 65; and Mary McLeod
Bethune, 70–71; biblical context
of, 67–68; biblical references,
88–89; as characteristic of God,
89; as female imagery, 69, 89;
Jesus as embodiment of, 68–69;
and Queen of Sheba, 72–87;
reflecting on, 88–89; as virtue,
67–71, 88–89; wisdom literature, 69

womanist ethic, 119–23
womanist theology, 117–19, 122
women's suffrage, 53, 54
works, and faith, 51–52
Wright, Jeremiah, 37–38

Zipporah: introduction, 37–38; justice reading strategy for, 40–41,
42–44; reflecting on, 46–47;
and salvation, 40–41; scripture
readings, 36, 46–47; story of,
38–40; traditional commentaries
on, 41–42